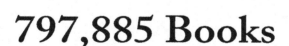

ISBN 978-1-333-45772-3
PIBN 10507022

1 MONTH OF
FREE
READING

at

www.ForgottenBooks.com

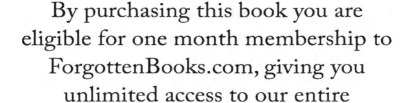

By purchasing this book you are eligible for one month membership to ForgottenBooks.com, giving you unlimited access to our entire collection of over 700,000 titles via our web site and mobile apps.

To claim your free month visit:
www.forgottenbooks.com/free507022

BROOKE'S 'ROMEUS AND JULIET' BEING THE ORIGINAL OF SHAKESPEARE'S 'ROMEO AND JULIET' NEWLY EDITED BY J. J. MUNRO

NEW YORK
DUFFIELD AND COMPANY
LONDON: CHATTO & WINDUS
1908

BROOKE'S 'ROMEUS AND JULIET' BEING THE ORIGINAL OF SHAKESPEARE'S 'ROMEO AND JULIET' NEWLY EDITED BY J. J. MUNRO

NEW YORK

DUFFIELD AND COMPANY

LONDON: CHATTO & WINDUS

1908

WEEVER'S SONNET, 1595.

Ad Gulielmum Shakespeare.

HONEY-TONGUED SHAKESPEARE, WHEN I SAW THINE ISSUE,
  I SWORE APOLLO GOT THEM AND NONE OTHER,
THEIR ROSY-TAINTED FEATURES CLOTHED IN TISSUE,
  SOME HEAVEN-BORN GODDESS SAID TO BE THEIR MOTHER:
ROSE-CHEEKED ADONIS WITH HIS AMBER TRESSES,
  FAIR FIRE-HOT VENUS CHARMING HIM TO LOVE HER,
CHASTE LUCRETIA VIRGIN-LIKE HER DRESSES,
  PROUD LUST-STUNG TARQUIN SEEKING STILL TO PROVE HER:
ROMEO, RICHARD, MORE, WHOSE NAMES I KNOW NOT,
  THEIR SUGARED TONGUES, AND POWER ATTRACTIVE BEAUTY
SAY THEY ARE SAINTS, ALTHOUGH THAT SAINTS THEY SHOW NOT,
  FOR THOUSANDS VOW TO THEM SUBJECTIVE DUTY:
THEY BURN IN LOVE THY CHILDREN, SHAKESPEARE, HET THEM,
GO, WOO THY MUSE MORE NYMPHISH BROOD BEGET THEM.

Epigrammes in the oldest cut, and newest fashion, etc.

EPIG. 22.

INTRODUCTION

General Consideration of the Story.—The Middle Ages have left us many tales of unhappy love, wherein the golden promise of youthful passion is transformed by unkindly circumstance into woe and death. Such tales were generally produced by a process of growth occupying many years and passing from land to land.

— Perhaps the most beautiful and tragic, certainly the most famous and highly developed of such old tales is the history of *Romeo and Juliet*. Its real origin is involved in much obscurity; but as Boswell[1] and Simrock[2] first pointed out, the story, in its principal elements, possesses striking analogy to the older love-tales of *Hero and Leander*, and *Pyramus and Thisbe*, and *Tristan and Isolde*. This analogy, however, should not be unduly pressed: it would be too much to say that its existence proves organic connexion between these stories, although an exceedingly remote relationship is possible; a number of other tales, like that of *Ulysses and Penelope*, possess too an analogy in some respects with *Romeo*, but can have no relation to it. Cino

---

[1] Boswell's Forewords to *Romeo and Juliet*, 1821, V. vi., p. 265.

[2] *Karl Simrock on the Plots of Shakespeare's Plays*, ed. *Halliwell Shak. Soc.*, 1850.

b

Chiarini[1] and Keightley[2] are two of those who are apt
to press the connexion too much, in considering *Pyramus
and Thisbe* as the ultimate source of the *Romeo* legend.
This theory of absolute relationship with one ancient
story is hardly tenable in the light of evidence which we
subsequently adduce, and the fact that the simple theme
of two distressed lovers would call forth the same type
of story in different minds, may explain some of the
similarity.

In -the three principal stories mentioned above, the
theme, on examination, is found to be the same and
consists of two main elements:

(*a*) the separation of two lovers by some obstacle;

(*b*) their ruin brought about by an error which
one holds in regard to the other, or by a
misfortune, which, happening to one, the
other shares.

Pyramus and Thisbe are separated by a wall; they
attempt to meet at the tomb of Ninus, where nothing shall
part them, but where Pyramus, thinking Thisbe dead,
slays himself; whereupon, Thisbe kills herself also. Hero
and Leander are parted by the Hellespont, which Leander
swims in order to reach Hero; Hero's guiding light is one

[1] *Romeo e Giulietta, La Storia Degli Amanti Veronesi nelle Novelle
Italiane e nella Tragedia di Shakespeare, novamente tradotta da Cino
Chiarini*, Firenze, 1906, pp. xix-xx. This book contains reprints of
Da Porto and Bandello.

[2] Furness's Variorum *Romeo*, p. 408.

night extinguished, and Leander loses heart and drowns; Hero drowns herself on the following morning on seeing his body washed ashore. Isolde and Tristan are parted by precepts of honour, Isolde being married to Mark; Tristan has, moreover, killed a kinsman of Isolde, and is therefore the natural enemy of her people; Isolde, however, goes to Tristan, but he dies through false news concerning her; Isolde herself dies on the body of her lover, seeing his sad fate.

Now taking *Tristan and Isolde*, the most northerly, and perhaps the most evolved of these tales (excepting *Romeo*), we see an advance on the other two: the obstacle between the lovers is no longer principally material, but is moral; and the slaying of the kinsman is a new and important feature. These developments are carried further in *Romeo*.

Besides these three old tales, however, there are two others not previously noticed in this connexion, and exceedingly popular in the Middle Ages, which also bear close analogy to *Romeo*; these are *Troilus and Cressida*, and *Floris and Blanchefleur*. The story of the first pair of lovers briefly is, that Troilus, who scorns love, sees Cressida, and falls in love with her. Troilus pines; his friend Pandarus comes to his aid with good counsel, and promises to win Cressida for him. Pandarus persuades Cressida, who pities Troilus, and finally consents to allow him to go to her bedside. They pass nights together, all their arrangements being made by the friendly Pandarus, their mutual messenger. Calchas, however, Cressida's father, has deserted Troy and joined the Greeks, and he prevails on his new friends to ask for the exchange of Cressida for their own Antenor. The parliament of Troy consents to this. The grief of the lovers at the prospect of this parting is uncontrollable, and each is comforted by the philosophic Pandarus. Troilus goes to Cressida at night for the last time and bids her farewell as the day begins to dawn. Troilus is afraid her father will desire to wed her to some other man; but Cressida swears constancy and promises to return in ten days. She is led to the Greek host by Diomedes, who loves her and woos her. His wooing is so successful that Cressida breaks her promise to Troilus and does not return. Letters pass between the lovers, and still Troilus hopes Cressida is true; till one day Deiphobus captures the armour of Diomedes and Troilus sees thereon the brooch he has given Cressida: thereupon he swears vengeance on Diomedes and seeks every day to fight with him, but is slain by Achilles. The parallelism between this story and *Romeo* is too apparent to require pointing out.

The romance of *Troilus and Cressida* is not of classical origin. The earliest version of it known to us is in *Le Roman de Troie*, by Benoît de Sainte-More,[1] a Norman poet of the French court of our English Henry II.[2] Other

---

[1] For a lengthy and able discussion of the Troilus story *see* M. A. Joly's *Benoît de Ste-More et le Roman de Troie*, Paris, 1870; and Jung's *Origin and Development of the Story of Troilus and Criseyde*, Chaucer Society, 1907.　　　　[2] Joly, p. 109.

poets had treated of the siege of Troy before him, but in his book first is the history of Troilus. M. Joly holds that he produced his long poem between 1175 and 1185, but the now accepted date is about 1160.[1] Benoît's work became speedily famous; the story became known in many lands, not only to the cultured people, but to the populace. It passed into histories and *gestes* and was a favourite theme of poets. Its glory was still further extended by a Latin *remaniement* of Benoît's poems by Guido delle Colonne of Messina, called the *Historia Destructionis Trojae*, written in 1287.[2] Guido's production became even more famous than Benoît's, and on the advent of printing, the presses of every land in Europe were soon actively reproducing his work.[3] When Boccaccio retold the story in his *Filostrato*, he gave it new life and significance. He took his main outlines from Guido and Benoît, but he owed little more to them. He wove into the history the joy and anguish, the sweetness and the bitterness, of his own love-affair —for he, too, had lost his love, the beautiful Maria, whom he called Fiammetta, and had met at the Neapolitan court of Queen Giovanna; and Jung shows, too, that his innovations are mainly due to borrowings from the early part of his own *Filocolo*, based on the medieval romance of *Floris and Blanchefleur*. Benoît had occupied

---

[1] *See* Jung, chap. I.

[2] *Testi Inediti di Storia Trojana* (4 vols.), by Egidio Gorra, Turin, 1887. *See* vol. i., pp. 105-6.

[3] Joly, p. 500.

himself chiefly with the feelings of Briseida (as Cressida
was then named); Boccaccio fixed attention chiefly on
Troilus. In Benoît and Guido there was no Pandarus;
Boccaccio was solely responsible for his creation.

The great Italian version of *Floris and Blanchefleur* is
Boccaccio's *Filocolo*. I shall notice chiefly here the points
which most interest us. Florio (Floris) was the son of
King Felice of Spain who had killed Lelio, a Roman noble,
husband to Giulia and father to Biancofiore (Blanchefleur),
born after his death. Biancofiore was brought up with
Florio at Felice's court and as the king noticed the growing
love between the two young people, he sent his son away to
Duke Feramonte in Montorio (corresponding to Mantua).
The Duke tried unsuccessfully to turn the young man's
thoughts from Biancofiore, who, meanwhile, had been
induced by the king, through his steward, to serve the
guests at a banquet with a poisoned pheasant, and had been
on that account condemned to be burnt. Florio was
warned by Venus and rescued Biancofiore. A rival to
Florio arose in Fileno; Florio became jealous, and would
have killed him, had he not fled. Felice then sent
Biancofiore away by merchants, who sold her to the
Admiral, and she was put in a tower at Alexandria.
Felice then made a sumptuous tomb and gave out that
Biancofiore was dead. Florio went to the sepulchre and
lamented bitterly, and wished for death; his mother, however,
told him the truth, and he went in search of Biancofiore,
eventually finding her and passing through many adventures.

The noticeable points are the name Giulia, the mention of Alexandria (cf. Masuccio Salernitano, later), the rivalry of the two families, the banishment of the hero, the incorrect publication of the heroine's death, and the hero's lamentations at the sepulchre. Whereas in *Troilus* the heroine was banished, the hero is banished in *Florio*; Diomed and Fileno correspond to Paris; Pandarus corresponds to Laurence.[1] The vacillation of Troilus and Cressida between joy and sorrow is the same as that of Romeo and Juliet; each pair pass the night together and bid farewell at morn; and both pairs are helped and comforted by the philosophical friend. It seems probable that these two stories, told by Boccaccio, passed, with others, into popular tales and gave rise to the legends which culminated in *Romeo*, and which, in their literary expression, came again under the direct influence of Boccaccio. Similar popular stories, which must have abounded in mediæval Italy, were widely circulated in different forms by such people as the archer Pellegrino of Da Porto,[2] and such evidence as we have tends to show that at an early date the *Romeo* legend was widespread in Italy. Masuccio Salernitano's story is told of Sienna, in Tuscany, and his book was printed in Naples; Da Porto, whose history refers to Verona, printed his book in Venice; Bandello's work was published in Lucca; and the scene of Groto's tragedy was laid in Adria.

---

[1] It should be remembered that the Nurse is a later development, due greatly to Brooke : the resemblance between *Troilus* and *Romeo* was, therefore, even greater in the earlier versions.   [2] *See* p. xxxi, below.

All those romances in which the great feature is separation leading to disastrous complications, I name "Separation" romances.

The source of the *Romeo* story, on one side, was probably, therefore, a "Separation" romance, or Separation romances, current in Italy, which, in common with *Troilus and Cressida* and *Florio and Biancofiore*, must have possessed :—

> (*a*) the meeting of two lovers, who, for some reason, probably the existence of a family feud, are obliged to keep their love secret;
>
> (*b*) a philosophical confidant who advises them and assists them to meet and helps them;
>
> (*c*) their betrothal;
>
> (*d*) their separation;
>
> (*e*) an affecting parting scene at dawning;
>
> (*f*) the advent of a new lover, who becomes a great danger to the hero and heroine;
>
> (*g*) disaster which ruins them.

In common with *Tristan and Isolde*,[1] the Separation romance or romances, must have possessed :—

> (*h*) the slaying of one of the heroine's kinsmen by the hero, thus producing (*d*) above;
>
> (*i*) an attempt made by one of the two to reach the other, probably in distress, perhaps on account of (*f*) above;

---

[1] It should be remembered that the *Tristan* story was well known in Italy in its Italian version.

(*j*) the ruin of the lovers, due to disaster, supposed or real, which has happened to one, again perhaps in connection with (*f*) above.

But in *Romeo* itself another series of new and important features is found, the actual marriage of the lovers, the subterfuge of the sleeping potion,[1] and the burial of the heroine in the sepulchre. This constitutes a distinct innovation in the cycle, and may well have been borrowed from some other source and added to the story. Luckily there exists a Middle Greek romance of the fifth century, in the *Ephesiaca* of Xenophon of Ephesus, which proves the existence of such a source: in this tale, Anthia, separated from her husband by misfortune, is rescued from robbers by Perilaus, who induces her, against her will, to consent to wed him; but she procures a poison (as she believes) from Eudoxus, a physician, and drinks it, in order to escape. She is buried in great pomp, but having merely swallowed a sleeping potion, awakes, and is carried off by thieves who plunder the sepulchre.[2] The notable features are that Anthia is already married, is separated from her husband, is forced to

---

[1] Sir B. W. Richardson experimented with some mandrake obtained from Greece, and the conclusion is that it must have been this mandrake wine that the friar gave Juliet in *Romeo*. This was called "death-wine" by the old Greeks, and they used it for surgical operations, as we use chloroform, a dose having the effect of causing apparent death.—*Daily News*, 23rd November, 1896.

See Note in Dr. Furnivall's Introduction to *Romeo*, *Century Shakspere*, and note Brooke's description of the making of Laurence's powder, ll. 2127-29.

[2] Dunlop's *History of Prose Fiction*, vol. i., p. 61 (ed. 1888).

consent to wed Perilaus, and, taking a potion, is buried as
if dead. Similar incidents to some of these occur in the
Babylonica of Iamblichus,[1] taken, as the author tells us, from
an Eastern book. Here Sinonis, beloved of Garmus, king
of Babylon, flies with her lover, Rhodanes ; the lovers sleep
one night in a sepulchre, and are thought to be corpses by
their pursuers ; Sinonis is seized by the magistrate, who
determines to send her to Babylon. The lovers provide
themselves with poison, but their guards, divining their
intention, substitute a soporific draught, which the lovers
swallow.[2] They awake from their sleep near Babylon.
Sinonis stabs herself, but not mortally.[3]

[1] Dunlop, p. 16, *seq.*

[2] According to some Russian versions of the Solomon story, Salomonia
is faithless, takes a narcotic and simulates death ; she is buried and dis-
interred, and is then carried off by her paramour. (Dunlop, ii., p. 637.)

[3] Most of these incidents passed into Italian novels, and were used
by Boccaccio. In his *Decameron* (Day 3, Novel 8), he tells the story of
a certain Ferondo, who, taking a drug, was buried as if dead and was
put into a dungeon. There he awoke and was led to believe he was in
purgatory. The story of Girolamo and Salvestre (Day 4, Novel 8) also
resembles the story of Romeo, and the story of Gentil de' Carisendi and
the wife of Niccoluccio is that of a woman who is buried as if dead.
Her lover opens her vault at night and lies by her side. She recovers
while he is there, and, after residing some time in his house, is restored
to her husband. (Day 10, Novel 4.)

A similar story to this, and more nearly approaching *Romeo*, is contained
in the thirteenth question discussed before Fiammetta in *Filocolo*. A
certain man had a fair wife who was loved by a knight, but who did not
love him. The knight was called away to a neighbouring city : while
there a messenger came and told him the lady was dead, and had been
buried by her relatives. He resolved to kiss her dead form. After dusk
he entered the city with one of his servants and made his way to the

The romances of the *Ephesiaca* and *Babylonica* type are also Separation romances of a kind, but their distinguishing feature is the subterfuge of the sleeping potion. On the success or failure of that everything depends. These romances I therefore call " Potion " romances.

A second source of the *Romeo* story, therefore, was a Potion romance, or Potion romances, which possessed :—

(*a*) two lovers, probably married, whose relations are endangered by

(*b*) the advent of a new lover ;

(*c*) the subterfuge of the sleeping potion obtained from

(*d*) a physician or friend ;

(*e*) the burial of the heroine, as if dead,

(*f*) and probably the forcing open of the tomb by the hero at night.

The coalition of the Separation and Potion romances was a simple process. The composite story would run as follows : [1]

S = Separation ; P = Potion.

1. S (*a*)
2. S (*b*) = P (*d*)
3. S (*c*)

sepulchre. Telling his servant to wait, he entered the tomb and embraced the lady. He soon found some signs of life in her. He and his servant carried her to his house, wrapped in his mantle. She was subsequently returned to her husband.

[1] I give this analysis at some length as it disposes of the frequent contention that the Romeo story is historical.

4. S (*h*)
5. S (*d*)
6. S (*e*) (together with the ladder incident, probably foreign to these sources).
7. S (*f*) = P (*b*)
8. P (*c*)
9. P (*e*)
10. P (*f*) = S (*i*)
11. S (*g*) and S (*j*)

As for the ladder incident, others occur in Ariosto's *Orlando Furioso*, Book 5, in the story of Ginevra and Lurcanio,[1] and again in our Matteo Bandello's novel of *Timbreo di Cardona and Fenicia Lionata*,[2] though here the ladder is of wood.

Even in its earliest known form the history of *Romeo and Juliet* was pathetic and beautiful; dealing as it did with the ruin of a glorious youth dominated by the eternal and elemental passion of mankind, it could hardly have been otherwise: but the glamour and the immortality which it possesses to-day it owes to our and all men's Shakspere, who adopted it, and vitalised it by infusing into it a lyric rapture and youthful ecstasy. The tale was already well known when he touched it with his genius, not only in

---

[1] *See* Harington's translation, reprinted by Furness, in his *Variorum Much Ado about Nothing*, p. 296.

[2] *See* John Payne's translation for the Villon Society, reprinted by Furness, *ib.*, p. 311.

England,[1] but in most of the countries of Europe,[2] and had already been employed for dramatic treatment: but its popularity in this country was mainly due to the poem of Arthur Brooke, which forms the text of our volume, and from which Shakspere drew most of the materials for his play.

The Author of the Poem.—Of Arthur Brooke himself we know very little: our interest in him must always be principally due to his connexion with Shakspere. For us the great work and distinguishing feature of his life is his *Tragicall Historye of Romeus and Iuliet;* and he has left us little else. From his denunciation of the friars and their ways in his introduction "To the Reader," and from his other known volume on Scripture, we may see that he was a zealous Protestant. His words (ll. 903-4),

> " I grant that I envy the bliss they livéd in;
> Oh, that I might have found the like, I wish it for no sin,"—

have been thought to signify that their writer was unmarried: probably he was; but these words, in all likelihood, owe their existence to another cause, not previously known, which we shall discuss later,[3] and they may be taken

---

1 *Philotimus*, published in 1583, mentions the story; Thomas Delapeend gives its argument in his *Pleasant Fable of Hermaphroditus and Salmacis,* 1565; Rich, in his *Dialogue between Mercury and a Soldier,* 1574, tells us that the tragedy was figured on tapestry, so widely was it known; and Austin Saker mentions it in his *Narbonus,* 1580.

2 Due greatly to the work of Da Porto and Bandello.

3 *See* Appendix II.

as poetical sentiment employed merely to intensify the description of the lovers' happiness. The other known book by our author is one entitled, "The Agreement of Sondry places of Scripture, seeming in shew to Jarre [jar], Seruing in stead of Commentaryes, not onely for these, but others lyke, Translated out of French, and nowe fyrst publyshed by Arthure Broke. Lucas Harrison, 1563." The printer tells us that the Author was absent from London at the time of printing, and could not, therefore, see the work through the press, and that he had been prevailed upon to leave this book behind him, "Worthy in deede, for lawfull and vnspotted doctrine, to beare his Syres Name : howbeit, yet rough [on account of the author's absence], vnmete to match with many other his trauaylles, satisfieng the hygh expectation that fame had blowen of hym." On fol. 308 are some verses by "Thomas Broke, the younger, to the Reader," wherein their author, after saying that joy cannot add one minute to life, continues :

> "Example, lo, in Broke before thine eye,
>   Whose praiséd gifts in him did late abound,
>   By shipwrack forced, alas, too soon to die,
>   Helpless of all intombed lies underground."

Brooke was, therefore, drowned in 1563, one year after the publication of his *Romeus*. His name and his poem seem to have speedily become well known. George Turbervile in his *Epitaphs, Epigrams, Songs and Sonnets, etc.*, 1570, has (pp. 143 b.-144 b.) a valuable poem in memory of our author, which, as it does not appear to have been given in full before, save in Collier's scarce reprint of Turbervile, is printed here :

"An Epitaph on the death of Master Arthur Brooke, drowned in passing to Newhaven [*i.e.*, Havre].

> "At point to end and finish this my Book,
> Came good report to me, and willed me write
> A doleful verse, in praise of Arthur Brooke,
> That age to come lament his fortune might.
>   Agreed, quoth I, for sure his virtues were
> As many as his years in number few :
> The Muses him in learned laps did bear,
> And Pallas' dug this dainty Bab did chew.
>   Apollo lent him lute for solace' sake
> To sound his verse by touch of stately string,
> And of the never fading bay[1] did make
> A laurel crown, about his brows to cling,
>   In proof that he for metre did excel,
> As may be judged by Juliet and her mate :
> For there he showed his cunning passing well
> When he the tale to English did translate.
>   But, what? as he to foreign realm was bound,
> With others moe his sovereign queen to serve,
> Amid the seas unlucky youth was drowned,
> More speedy death than such one did deserve.
>   Ay me, that time, thou crooked Dolphin,[2] where
> Wast thou, Arion's help and only stay,
> That safely him from sea to shore didst bear?
> When Brooke was drowned why wast thou then away?
>   If sound of harp thine ear delighted so
> And causer was that he bestrid thy back,
> Then doubtless thou moughtst well on Brooke bestow

---

1 *Original*, Bayde.   2 *O.*, Delphin.

As good a turn to save him from the wrack.
   For sure his hand Arion's harp excelled,
His pleasant pen did pass the other's skill,
Whoso his book with judging eye beheld
Gave thanks to him and praised his learned quill.
   Thou cruel Gulf, what meanst thou to devour
With supping seas a jewel of such fame?
Why didst thou so with water mar the flower,
That Pallas thought so curiously to frame?
   Unhappy was the haven which he sought,
Cruel the seas whereon his ship did glide,
The winds so rough that Brooke to ruin brought,
Unskilful he that undertook to guide. [1]
   But sithens tears can not revoke the dead,
Nor cries recall a drownéd man to land :
Let this suffice t' extol [2] the life he led
And print his praise in house of Fame to stande,
    That they that after us shall be and live
    Deservéd praise to Arthur Brooke may give."

We are able to give for the first time some account of the circumstances under which Brooke was drowned: *see* Appendix III.

Brooke, in his lines to the Reader, and Lucas Harrison in the Scriptural volume, speak of other works from Brooke's pen, but we know nothing of them. Turbervile's lines establish his authorship of *Romeus*, and his youth when he so unhappily died.

Date of the Poem.—Brooke's statement "The eldest of them, lo, I offer to the stake, my youthful work"

---

1 *O., again* glide.   2 *O.,* extal.

(To the Reader, p. lxvii.), with its context, have been thought to imply that his poem was an early production, which, later in life, he published, and for whose imperfections he desired to apologise; but such a hypothesis will not bear investigation. The immediate original of the poem was Boaistuau's *Histoires Tragiques*; and this was not published until 1559: Brooke's poem appeared in 1562; and the author could only have been referring to his *present* youth in the above statement. We know, too, from Turbervile that Brooke was very young when he died.

Originals and Sources.—Considerable controversy has raged round the authenticity of the *Romeo* legend. Alessandro Torri[1] and Filippo Scolari were both convinced of the historical reality of the story of the two unfortunate lovers. There is little evidence, however, to support their contention. We are told[2] that the sepulchral stone of Romeo and Juliet, from their tomb, was bought, at high price, by John, Archduke of Austria. Direct evidence, apart from this, except the statement that the lovers lived in the days of Bartolommeo Della Scala, there appears to be none. Early Italian historians, with a single exception to which we shall refer later, make no mention of our story; even Sarayna,[3] who, in 1542, published *Le Historie e fatti de' Veronesi nelli tempi del popolo e Signori Scaligeri*, and even

---

[1] In 1831 Torri published in Pisa his *Giulietta e Romeo*, etc., nowadays, as Chiarini tells us, a rare book, wherein he reprinted the novels of Da Porto and Bandello, the poem of Clitia and other old compositions connected with the *Romeo* tale. Scolari was his friend.

[2] Chiarini, p. xii.   [3] Chiarini, p. xii.; Furness, *cit.* Singer, p. 399.

speaks of the time of Bartolommeo Della Scala and mentions other Domestic tragedies, does not refer to it. The often-quoted lines from the sixth canto of Dante's *Purgatorio*, l. 106 :

> " Vieni a veder Montecchi e Cappelletti,
> Monaldi e Filippeschi, uom sensa cura !
> Color già tristi, e costor con sospetti," 1

which have long been considered as referring to the rival parties of the *Romeo* story, cannot be held to be in any way connected. Dante's *Capulets and Montagues* were both component parts of the same Ghibelline party, and were both more or less reduced in circumstances through the neglect of the emperor Albert. Chiarini points out, more-over, that there is no record of a family of Capulets in Verona, and adds that, probably, what was originally the name of a political faction, became at a later date the surname of a family.

There may or may not have been a Romeo and a Juliet by name, and they may or may not have been unfortunate lovers, but the facts above-mentioned and our previous analysis of their legend, render it extremely improbable that any part of their history, as we have it, can be true, except, perhaps, if they lived at all, their burial together.

The earliest tale we know containing the elements of the Veronese legend is Masuccio Salernitano's romance of

---

1 Translated by Cary :—
  " Come see the Capulets and Montagues,
    The Filippeschi and Monaldi, man,
    Who car'st for nought ! Those sunk in grief, and these
    With dire suspicion rack'd."

Mariotto Mignanelli of Sienna and Giannozza Saracini, the thirty-third novel of his *Cinquante Novelle,* published in Naples in 1476.[1] In it Mariotto loved Giannozza, and could not marry her publicly; an Augustine monk was, therefore, bribed to wed them in secret. Mariotto subsequently struck a fellow-citizen in fight, so that the man died, and he was condemned by the Podestà to banishment. After asking his brother, Gargano, to keep him informed of affairs in Sienna, he went to his uncle Nicolo Mignanelli, a merchant in Alexandria. Giannozza was, meanwhile, being urged by her angry father to wed, and in order to evade this, conceived the idea of pretending death. She bribed the friar to compound her a sleeping potion which should cause her to sleep for three days: this she drank, was taken for dead, and was buried in the church of St. Augustine. She had previously written of her intentions to Mariotto, but her messenger and his ship were seized by pirates and her letter was lost. Mariotto's brother informed him by letter of her supposed death, and the unhappy lover returned to Sienna, determined to die at his wife's tomb. The friar had already removed her body, but Mariotto not knowing this, attempted to force open the vault, was seized in so doing, was recognised, racked and decapitated. Giannozza, disguised as a man, had meanwhile gone to Alexandria and heard of her

---

[1] *See* Daniel, *Romeus and Juliet,* etc., New Shakspere Society, 1875, p. iv.; Chiarini, p. xxi.; Furness's *Variorum Romeo and Juliet* (from Simrock), p. 399.

husband's departure; she returned to Sienna, to find he
had been beheaded three days before. She retired to a
nunnery and died broken-hearted.[1] Masuccio calls on
God to witness that all his tales happened in his own
times.

Whether Luigi Da Porto's *Historia novellamente ritrovata
di due nobili amanti*,[2] etc. (Venice *c.* 1530) was founded on
Masuccio Salernitano's tale or not is uncertain: Da Porto's
story may have been (and probably was) an independent
record of the same legend. It contains the first mention of
Romeo and Juliet; and various editions of it were published
during the sixteenth century. Da Porto says that the
lovers lived in the days of Bartolommeo Della Scala, that
Romeo was already in love and followed his cruel mistress to
the feast of Antonio Cappelletti, disguised as a nymph;
here he beheld Juliet, and for her at once forgot his old
love. The lovers sat together after a dance, Marcuccio
Guercio (Mercutio) with them, and spoke[3]: they met at night
at Juliet's window and their love increased. They resolved

---

1 That this was probably but one recorded form of a popular legend
which became localised in different places, and of which there were
slightly different versions, is supported by the difference between the
Argument and the conclusion of the tale. In the novel Giannozza
retires to a nunnery and dies : in the *Argument* she dies of grief on the
body of her lover : "La donna no'l trova in Allessandria, ritorna a
Siena, e trova l'amante decollato, e ella sopra il suo corpo per dolore si
muore." Note that in *Romeo* Laurence offers to find Juliet a nunnery,
but that she dies on her lover's body.

2 Chiarini's reprint, p. 1 ; Daniel's epitome, p. 5.

3 Chiarini's reprint, p. 7.

on secret marriage, and Friar Lorenzo was induced to wed
them.   Shortly after this occurred a street-fight in which
Romeo, after hesitation, attacked Tebaldo Cappelletti
(Tybalt) in anger, and slew him ; Romeo was then banished
for ever from Verona, and took leave of Juliet at the
friar's cell,[1] leaving Lorenzo and Juliet's servant (Pietro ;
Shakspere's Peter) to inform him of all news, and hoping to
get his banishment repealed.   Juliet broke down in grief,
and her parents were led to believe that marriage alone
could help their daughter, who was then about eighteen
years old.[2] Thereupon they commenced arrangements with
a count of Lodrone (later, Paris) to that end.   This was
told to Juliet by her mother, Giovanna,[3] but the daughter
expressed disapproval of the match to both her parents, and
said she would rather marry a Montague or die, than wed the
chosen Paris ; thus arousing her father's anger.   She sent
this intelligence through Pietro to Romeo, who replied, desir-
ing her still to maintain their mutual secret.   The threats of
Antonio drove her to consult Friar Lorenzo, who for the
sake of Romeo's friendship, and to prevent open scandal,
gave her a powder (una polvere) which would cause her to
lie as if dead for forty-eight hours.[4] She would then be
buried in the tomb of the Cappelletti, and he could carry
her to his cell where she might remain till she could escape,
disguised as a monk, to Mantua.   Meanwhile he would

---

1 Chiarini's reprint, p. 15.   2 *Ib.*, p. 17.
3 *Ib.*, p. 18.   4 *Ib.*, p. 23.

send a letter which she was to write to Romeo, by a brother, telling him of their doings. Juliet took the powder, returned home and professed submission to her father. At night she asked one of her servants for a cup of cold water, to refresh her, and mixing the potion, drank it, declaring in the presence of the servant and her aunt: Mio padre per certo contra mio volere non mi dara marito, s'io potrò.[1] The friar's messenger was, meanwhile, ineffectually trying to reach Romeo. In the morning Juliet was found on her bed, apparently dead; and afterwards, with great mourning, was laid in the family vault. Pietro, not being able to meet Lorenzo, who had left the city for a time, departed to Mantua and informed Romeo that Juliet was dead. Romeo paled and became like a dead man,. and drew his sword to kill himself,[2] but was restrained by Pietro, whom he finally dismissed, giving him a brown garment that he had. He resolved to return to Verona, and departed disguised as a peasant (contadino), taking with him a small bottle of poison (una guastadetta d'acqua di serpe) that he had in a chest. He arrived unnoticed in Verona at night, opened the vault, and with the aid of his lantern beheld the body of Juliet, whom he addressed in sorrow; he then swallowed his poison, and embracing his love, awaited death.[3] The strength of the powder was now decreasing, and Juliet soon awoke and speedily discovered in whose arms she lay, having at first thought that

---

1 Chiarini's reprint, p. 25.   2 *Ib.*, p. 29.
3 *Ib.*, p. 32.

Lorenzo had wronged her. The lovers mingled their lamentations and expressions of affection. Lorenzo at this point, knowing the virtue of the powder would fail about then, arrived with his faithful companion, and saw the two lovers. Romeo died and Juliet called for a knife to kill herself. The friar promised to find her a place in some holy convent;[1] Juliet, however, held her breath for a good time, and finally, with a great cry, expired on her lover's body. The watch arrived and seeing the light and hearing the noise, interrogated Lorenzo; the friar extinguished the light, closed the tomb and refused to answer their questions. The Cappelletti were apprised, and the prince was constrained to hold an enquiry. Lorenzo equivocated, but the tomb was opened by his fellow monks, and the truth revealed. The rival families were then reconciled, and the lovers were buried together with great ceremony.[2] In his *Forewords* Da Porto tells us that he learnt the tale in his soldier days from a Veronese archer named Pellegrino, like all his townsmen, a fine talker, and an expert soldier. Da Porto's narrative very speedily became widely known, and apparently travelled to France. Adrian Sevin's History of Burglipha and Halquadrich (1541-2) appears to be an echo or imitation of it. It could hardly have been independent. It possesses little interest for Shakspere students.[3]

---

[1] Chiarini's reprint, p. 35.   [2] *Ib.*, p. 40.
[3] For an epitome, *see* Daniel, p. viii.

The next Italian version of *Romeo* after Dá Porto was a
poem entitled, *L'Infelice Amore dei due Fedelissimi Amanti
Giulia e Romeo,* written by Clitia (or Clizia) to her Ardeo (1553),
and published by Giolito in Venice. The "authoress" and
her Ardeo cannot now be properly identified, but conjecture
has it that the poem was written by Gherardo Bolderi.[1] Clitia
states at the start that 150 years had passed since the
Capulets and the Montagues, of old at feud, had forgotten
somewhat their enmity and the *Romeo* story began. If
then the date which Da Porto and Bandello assign to
the tragedy be accepted (1301-4), the date of Clitia's
composition must be about 1453. This would make
Clitia the earliest *Romeo* record; but considerations of
style do not point to so early a date; considerations of
text lead to the belief that Clitia followed Da Porto; and
it is highly improbable that the MS. could have lain 100
years before publication. Filippo Scolari[2] supposes that
Clitia wrote little previous to publication. Although Clitia's
version follows Da Porto, it differs in several particulars :—
(1) Lady Capulet here first supposes Tybalt's death to be
the cause of Juliet's sorrow after Romeo's banishment. (2)
Romeo does not attempt his life on hearing of Juliet's sup-
posed death. (3) He gives Pietro a gold chain (instead of
a garment, as before) on dismissing him, and sends him to
tell the Friar of his coming. (4) Pietro does not do this,

---

[1] Chiarini, p. xviii.

[2] *Su la pietosa morte di G. Cappelletti e R. Montecchi. Lettere Critiche
de Filippo Scolari,* Livorno, 1831, p. 37.

and is no more heard of. (5) Romeo dies in Juliet's arms before the Friar arrives, who (6) comes to the tomb alone. (7) The poem then ends abruptly with Juliet's death.[1]

After Clitia came Matteo Bandello with his Novello of *Giulietta e Romeo* published in Lucca in 1554 in the second of his three volumes. Dedicated to Girolamo Fracastro, Bandello, in the main, follows Da Porto, whose narrative he enlarges and ornaments,[2] but he appears also to have borrowed from Clitia. In Bandello the story approaches yet more to its Shaksperian form. Romeo's first love-affair is here dwelt upon, and he goes to the Capulet feast, not to pursue his cruel lady, but on the advice of a friend to behold other beauties.[3] He goes masked, but not as a nymph (as in Da Porto). Here, too, we first meet the Nurse, from whom Juliet learns Romeo's identity.[4] The Nurse carries messages between the lovers, and the parting takes place at the heroine's house. The county is now called Paris, conte di Lodrone;[5] the Friar is named Lorenzo da Reggio;[6] and Pietro (in Da Porto, Juliet's servant) becomes Romeo's man. Juliet drinks the potion in secret,[7] and is thought to have died of grief.[8] Lorenzo's messenger is a friar named Anselmo, who, arriving at Mantua, goes to the

---

[1] Daniel, p. ix : this poem was printed by Torri. A description of Clitia's poem will be found in *The Shakspere Society's Papers*, 1849, Vol. iv., Art. ii.

[2] *Nelle sue* [Bandello's] *mani l'arido racconto del Da Porto, così spesso monotono e scolorito si allarga e si avviva.*—Chiarini, p. xxv.

[3] Chiarini's reprint, p. 52.   [4] *Ib.*, p. 59.   [5] *Ib.*, p. 76.
[6] *Ib.*, p. 63..   [7] *Ib.*, p. 89.   [8] *Ib.*, p. 91.

Franciscan monastery there, to get a companion, and is there detained in consequence of death through plague.[1] Pietro here first acquaints his master with news of Juliet's supposed death, having seen her carried to the sepulchre,[2] and is sent back to Verona to provide instruments for opening the tomb.[3] Romeo writes to his father the whole story in a letter, settles his affairs, and taking the poison with him,[4] he sets out on horse, disguised as a German,[5] for Verona, where he meets Pietro. They go to the tomb at night; Romeo gives his man his letter, and tells him he obtained the poison from a certain Spolentino in Mantua,[6] and directs him to close the sepulchre. He then takes the poison, and embracing Juliet, awaits death. Juliet then awakes, and seeing a figure by her in a German costume is startled, and thinks Lorenzo has betrayed her.[7] She soon discovers it is her Romeo. The lovers mutually lament and express their love. Romeo asks forgiveness of the dead Tebaldo.[8] Lorenzo, with another friar, now comes to the sepulchre, and meeting Pietro, asks concerning Romeo, while Romeo himself is dying. Lorenzo beholds the lovers, and offers to find Juliet a nunnery, as before; but she dies on the body of her lover. The two friars and Pietro think she has fainted and try to revive her, when the watch arrive[9] and arrest them. Barto-

---

[1] Chiarini's reprint, p. 93.   [2] *Ib.,* p. 95.   [3] *Ib.,* p. 98.
[4] "un' ampoletta piena d'acqa velenosissima," *Ib.,* p. 99, but afterwards described as in Da Porto: "l'acqua, che del serpe l'uom appella," p. 111; *see* also p. 101.
[5] *Ib.,* p. 100.   [6] *Ib.,* p. 101.   [7] *Ib.,* p. 103.
[8] *Ib.,* p. 105.   [9] *Ib.,* p. 110.

Iommeo examines them on the affair, and they are pardoned. The Capulets and Montagues make peace, and the lovers are buried together in great pomp. The Novello concludes with the lovers' epitaph.[1]

Bandello's tale speedily acquired a greater popularity than Da Porto's : it was translated by Boaistuau (or Boisteau) in his *Histoires Tragiqves, Extraictes des Oeuvres Italiennes de Bandel, & mises en nostre langue Françoise, par Pierre Boaistuau surnommé Launay, natif de Bretaigne*, Paris, 1559. Here it forms the *Histoire Troisiesme, De deux amans, dont l'vn mourut de venin, l'autre de tristesse* (p. 39). Boaistuau in his *Advertissement au Lecteur* begs the reader not to find it ill that he has not closely followed Bandello's style, which he considers rude and meagre, and says that he has recast all afresh. One is not able to concur with Boaistuau in his opinion as to Bandello, but the important point is that in his recasting he made various changes, which contribute in the development towards Shakspere. The scene with the Apothecary is expanded from Bandello's hint.[2] Romeo's man and Laurens arrive after Romeo's demise, while Juliet still sleeps, a circumstance which may be due to influence of Clitia, or to another version of the legend. Juliet refuses to leave the tomb. When the servant and friar withdraw on hearing a noise, Juliet stabs herself with Romeo's dagger. Laurens and his companion are arrested

---

1 *Ib.*, p. 111. *See* Daniel's epitome, which I used for basis, p. x.
2 *Boaistuau*, edition 1559, p. 76.

by the watch and imprisoned. The bodies are set out to view on a stage, and the Prince holds an enquiry. Laurens and the servant are pardoned; the Nurse is banished; the apothecary is racked and hanged; and the lovers are buried in a sumptuous tomb.

The story was now to have literary record in England, for from Boaistuau's *Histoire* Arthur Brooke made his poem, published in 1562, and Painter subsequently made his translation, published in his *Palace of Pleasure*, Vol. II., in 1567. Brooke's use of Boaistuau will be dealt with in the criticism of his book. A criticism of Painter follows.

This constitutes the direct line towards Shakspere; we have now to go back somewhat, and consider the more important literature, apart from the above versions, which had sprung from the Romeo legend.

The single exception among Italian historians who gives credence and record to the Romeo story is Girolamo delle Corte, who relates the tragedy in his *Storia di Verona* as actually happening in 1303; but as his account appeared for the first time in 1594, when Da Porto, Bandello, Boaistuau, Brooke, Painter, and Shakspere had already written their works, and when the legend had spread over Italy, it has no value whatever as history. Girolamo delle Corte appears to have merely accepted the popular tradition as circumstantial, and to have adopted it to enliven his work.

Concerning the blind poet Luigi Groto's *La Hadriana* (1578), a great deal has been written. In 1799, Joseph Cooper Walker published his *Historical Memoir on Italian*

Tragedy, in which he claimed that Shakspere was cognisant of Groto's play. W. W. Lloyd,[1] in Singer's *Shakspere*, added considerably to Walker's evidence, and, in our opinion, came one step nearer the truth, in inferring that Shakspere used some English adaptation of Groto. From a cursory examination, *La Hadriana* would appear to be simply a transference of the Romeo story to the " glorious city of Adria," of more ancient times, with frequent borrowings from Da Porto, on whose novel the plot appears to be based. Cino Chiarini, however, refers it to Bandello;[2] and the truth is that both novels seem to have contributed towards its construction. The consensus of critical opinion is that there is no connexion between Luigi Groto and Shakspere, and in consideration of this point the following analysis is made.

La Hadriana possesses in common with Da Porto and with no other Italian work: (1) The ironical statement that the heroine might rather wed their family enemy (a Montague or Latino) than him who has been chosen by her parents (Paris or the Sabine prince).[3] (2) The heroine's asking for water in the night to quench her thirst, but really to mix

---

[1] Furness, cit. Lloyd, p. 402, *seq.* An epitome of *La Hadriana* and an examination of Walker's and Lloyd's arguments is given in Daniel, pp. xxii.-xxxii., and of this epitome I make use in my examination. A thorough comparison between Groto's play and Shakspere's will be found in Giuseppe Chiarini's *Studi Shakspeariani*, Livorno, 1896, pp. 243-269.

[2] C. Chiarini, p. xxvi.

[3] Daniel's epitome, p. xxiv., and *see* p. xxxi ; our epitome of Da Porto, above, p. xxix.

her potion,[1] (3) her drinking it in the presence of the servant,[2] and (4) her statement before the servant that her father (Capulet or Mezentio) should not wed her that day.[3] (5) The gift by the hero of his cloak to the messenger who brought the news of the heroine's supposed death.

In common with Bandello, *La Hadriana* possesses: (1) The character of the Nurse as confidante and go-between.[4] (2) The parting of the lovers at the heroine's house, where the hero arrives by stealth.[5]

The conclusion in *La Hadriana*, however, is different from that in both Da Porto and Bandello; in Groto's tragedy, the heroine stabs herself, and the hero dies before the Mago arrives. This is precisely the ending in Boaistuau.[6]

Apart from these considerations, moreover, there are a number of particulars in which Groto's *Hadriana* agrees only with Shakspere's *Romeo*. These are:

(1) The hero's talk of his readiness to die in the parting scene with the heroine (in Groto, Latino offers his sword to

---

[1] Daniel, p. xxv.; our epitome, p. xxx.

[2] *Ib.*, p. xxv.; our epitome, p. xxx. It should be noted, however, that in Groto this servant is the Nurse, who corresponds to the Nurse in Bandello, and who, of course, saw her mistress to bed.

[3] *Ib.*, p. xxvi.; our epitome, p. xxx.

[4] *Ib.*, p. xxii., etc.; our epitome, p. xxxiii.

[5] *Ib.*, p. xxiii.; our epitome, p. xxxiii.

[6] *Ib*, p. xxvi.; above, p. xxxv. In Clitia, too, Romeo dies before Friar Tricastro (Laurence) arrives, but here, as in Da Porto, etc., Giulia dies by holding her breath.

Hadriana and puts his life in her hands).[1]   (2) The entry of
the Nurse at the conclusion of the parting scene.[2]   (3) Her
interference in the arranging of the second wedding (with
Paris or the Sabine prince).[3]   (4) The ironical words, in
one case by the mother to the daughter and in the other by
the daughter to the mother, that the daughter might rather
wed the enemy who has slain her kinsman (Romeo or Latino)
than her father's choice.[4]   (5) The consolation of the be-
reaved fathers (Capulet and Mezentino)—who, in these two
plays alone, give vent to their sorrow,—by a councillor (in
Romeo by Laurence), in both cases the idea being to console
the father with philosophical reflections.[5]   (6) The return of
the Friar's and the Mago's letters by their messengers.[6]
(7) The mention of both poisoning and stabbing at the
heroine's death,—in Groto's play, Hadriana tells the Mago
she has poisoned herself, and afterwards stabs herself; in
Shakspere Juliet chides dead Romeo for leaving none of
the poison, and also afterwards stabs herself.[7]

1 Daniel, p. xxiii.; Shakspere, III., v., 17.

2 *Ib.*, p. xxiii. ; Shakspere, III., v., 37.

3 *Ib.*, p. xxiv.; Shakspere, III., v., 169 and 214-227.

4 Mentioned before in reference to Da Porto, but as there can be no
direct connexion between Da Porto and Shakspere this case is cited;
Daniel, pp. xxiv.-xxxi.; Shakspere, III., v., 122.   There may be con-
nexion between the names *Latino* and *Romeo*.

  Daniel, p. xxv.; Shakspere, IV., v., 65-83.

6 *Ib.*, p. xxxi.; Shakspere, V., ii.

7 *Ib.*, p. xxvi.; Shakspere, V., iii., 161.   Note that Juliet calls
for a knife in Da Porto also, but does not die of poison.   *See* p. xxxi.
above.

Besides these cases there are verbal similarities and parallelisms of idea. When the lovers are parting in *La Hadriana*, Latino exclaims:

> " S'io non erro, e presso il far del giorno.
> Udite il rossignuol, che con noi desto,
> Con noi geme fra i spini, e la nigiada
> Col pianto nostro bagna l'herbe. Ahi lasso,
> Rivolgete la faccia a l'Oriente.
> Ecco incomincia a spuntar l'alba fuori,
> Portando un' altro sol sopra la terra,
> Che peró dal mio Sol resterà vinto."

> " If I err not, the lamp of day is nigh.
> List to the nightingale, that wakes with us,
> With us laments mid thorns; and now the dew,
> Like our tears, pearls the grass. Ah me, alas,
> Turn toward the east thy face.
> There now begins the morning to break forth,
> Bringing another sun above the earth
> That yet by my sun shall rest vanquished." [1]

Compare this with the parting of Romeo and Juliet, III., v. Similar resemblance was detected by Walker in the Mago's and the Friar's words to the heroine about the sleeping-potion, and in their speeches concerning their plans for the future.[2] W. W. Lloyd pointed out the resemblance between Latino's and Romeo's antithetical definition of love.[3] Daniel showed the resemblance between Latino and Romeo, in that they both address the sepulchre on going there to die, and queried a possible connexion

1 Daniel, p. xxvii.   2 *Ib.*, p. xxviii.
3 *Ib.* ; Furness, cit. Lloyd, p. 402.

between the two Nurses' references to the childhood of the heroines.[1] The majority of these incidents in Shakspere were certainly not taken from Brooke.

Whatever the reason of this curious similarity may be, there can be no doubt that it exists. Individual instances may not be convincing, but taken as a whole, these cases of very apparent relationship form an argument which may not be brushed aside without great consideration.

Now, viewing the evidence before us, it becomes apparent that Groto either made use of Da Porto, Bandello, and Boaistuau, all three, or borrowed from some third Italian source a novel or play, now unknown, which led Boaistuau to alter his ending, and which was based on, or similar to, Da Porto and Bandello. Similar as Groto's tragedy is in general outline to the *Romeo* story, an examination reveals the absence of many significant incidents and shows a difference of treatment, and the play seems to be too distantly removed from the story of the Italian novels to warrant the assumption of immediate connexion with them; and it is highly improbable, too, that Groto made use of Boaistuau. If then, as seems likely, there was a third Italian version of the *Romeo* story, other than Clitia, it must have been some adaptation or translation of this, which, apart from Brooke, influenced Shakspere.[2] In this way, and in this way only,

---

1 Daniel, pp. xxx.-xxxi.

2 There appears to be no evidence that Groto's tragedy was known in England at the time of the composition of *Romeo*, and even though it were, it is hard to believe that it could have been associated with that

d

can we explain the similarities between *La Hadriana* and *Romeo*, and the fact that Shakspere's tragedy reverted in two particulars to the plot as found in Da Porto,—in the heroine's ironical words to her mother that she would rather wed a Montague than Paris, and in Peter's position as servant to Juliet (in Bandello, etc., he became Romeo's man).

From this we pass to the Dutch play of *Romeo en Juliette*, written in Alexandrine couplets by Jacob Struijs in 1630, but not published till 1634.[1] The text in Struijs is based to a large extent on the prose of Boaistuau, but at many points it departs from that version and coincides with Shakspere in incidents which the English dramatist did not obtain from Brooke.

Struijs agrees with Boaistuau in: (*a*) the names of the characters; (*b*) large portions of the dialogue; (*c*) Juliette's comments on Thibout's death and Romeo's deed; (*d*) Capellet's words to Juliette on her refusal to accept Paris; (*e*) in the incident of the fray which proved fatal to Thibout; and in many other points.[2]

Struijs agrees exclusively with Brooke in the incident in which Juliet deceives the Nurse. In the Dutch play and

play. Ben Jonson mentioned *La Hadriana* in his *Volpone*, produced in 1605, and although Florio mentioned it in his list of *Authors and Books*, etc., 1611, he omitted it from his earlier list in 1598. (*See* Daniel, p. xxxi.)

[1] See *Romeo and Juliette*, by Harold de Wulf Fuller, reprinted from *Modern Philology*, July, 1906.

[2] Fuller, pp. 2, 3.

Brooke it comes after Juliet's visit to Laurence (ll. 2288-2316); in Shakspere it occurs immediately after the expression of Capulet's wrath (III. v. 213-242); in Boaistuau and Painter there is no such conversation.[1]

Struijs agrees exclusively with Shakspere or resembles him in the following points:

(*a*) There is great similarity in the two plays in Romeo's description of Juliet at the feast,[2] (*b*) in the incident of the first night meeting in the moonlight,[3] (*c*) in the opening of the scene where Laurence is discovered in front of his cell, before the entry of Romeo,[4] and (*d*) in Tybalt's desire to attack Romeo at the feast.[5] (*e*) They agree in the main features of the fray in which Mercutio (in Struijs called Phebidas) and Tybalt were killed,[6] (and although the general outline is the same there is great difference in language and treatment). (*f*) They agree in the fact that Romeo lamented over his misfortunes in the cell of Laurence,[7] and in the entry of the Nurse at that time. (*g*) They resemble each other in the parting of the lovers.[8]

Here, again, we are presented with the same alternatives as in the case of Luigi Groto and the Italian novelists,

---

1 Fuller, pp. 4-6; this is not the only point in which Brooke and Struijs agree, as against Boaistuau, as we show later, pp. xlv., liii.-iv., lvii.

2 *Ib.*, p. 7.   3 *Ib.*, p. 8.   4 *Ib.*, p. 9.

5 *Ib.*, p. 10, but in Struijs, Thibout recounts this afterwards, and says he refrained for fear of dishonouring the company.

6 *Ib.*, p. 12.

7 *Ib.*, pp. 13-14; we return to this later, as it occurs also in Brooke.

8 *Ib.*, pp. 15-16.

either that Struijs used Boaistuau and Brooke and Shakspere, or that he used Boaistuau for basis and some now lost composition which influenced alike Brooke's poem and Shakspere's play.

Now it becomes very apparent in several ways that Struijs did not pilfer Shakspere. He omits connecting Paris with the final catastrophe, following Boaistuau in this as in the three nocturnal meetings between the lovers, and he lacks that perfect tightening-up and compression of time characteristic of Shakspere's play. In a very able chapter Mr. Fuller examines the striking verbal similarities between the two dramatists, and points out, what is very apparent, that the text of Struijs seems in no way a copying of Shakspere, but rather, in the points of resemblance, like a cruder and more prolix original which gave rise to the stronger and more concentrated utterances of the English poet. What seems a mere hint in Struijs is worked out with dramatic beauty in Shakspere, and small incidents in the latter like the fear of Paris' page and the sleeping of Balthasar in the churchyard have their counterpart in Struijs, where Pedro, Romeo's man, is afraid of ghosts and sits down to sleep. Moreover, the Nurse, in Struijs is not a comic character,[1] which she most certainly would be had Struijs followed Shakspere.

Apparently, then, Struijs did not use Shakspere, and the only other explanation left to us, is that the latter himself

[1] Fuller, pp. 19-20. I have not space to note all Mr. Fuller's examples: these may suffice.

made use of an original accessible also to the former. It becomes apparent, too, that such an 'original' antedated Brooke, firstly, because Brooke must have borrowed from it in the Nurse's advice to Juliet to wed Paris, and in Romeo's lamentations at the friar's cell,[1] and secondly, because the 'original' did not take from Brooke the comic character of the Nurse or Romeo's sorrow when separated from Juliet, the former of which was, as Mr. Fuller says, "gratuity for any dramatist." In fixing the date of this 'original,' which must have been English, Mr. Fuller places it between 1559 (the date of Boaistuau's *Histoires*) and 1562 (the date of Brooke), apparently inferring that this 'original' was based on Boaistuau, and hence explaining the debt of Struijs to the latter. I see no reason to support this view. The Boaistuau passage in Struijs, given by Mr. Fuller himself, is so similar to its original that one is forced to believe that Struijs borrowed either from the French Novelist direct, or from his early Dutch translation; and as Shakspere employed both Brooke and the 'original' in composing his play, so Struijs may have used Boaistuau and the 'original' in composing his. These considerations lead to important conclusions. They mean that the earlier 'original' was not necessarily founded on Boaistuau, although its date could not have been many years prior to 1562.[2]

---

1 Fuller, p. 22 ; *see* pp. xliii., liii.-iv., lvii.

2 Brooke says he "lately" saw the "same argument" set forth on the stage, and considering the condition of the English drama prior to

Mr. Fuller concludes that this lost 'original' was a play, firstly, because Brooke says that there was an earlier play on this subject, and secondly, because this type of literature could most easily have travelled to Holland through the agency of an English theatrical company. We know that Brooke borrowed from some source other than Boaistuau, and that he says he saw an earlier play on *Romeo*; but the evidence for Mr. Fuller's absolute contention is very scanty. Were the 'original' certainly a play, one would expect to find resemblance between Shakspere and Struijs in the arrangement of scenes, but it is difficult to discover any such resemblance, the means adopted by the one to further the action are, at different points, distinct from those adopted by the other. What happened at the feast has, in Struijs, to be told in narrative by Romeo and Thibout, and one scene is given up to Romeo's farewell to Verona. Notwithstanding this, however, the supposition that the lost link is a play, is probably correct; but one must insist, in regard to the paucity of the evidence, that this is not certain.

Here, then, we are led to believe again that there was a source from which Shakspere drew, other than Brooke; and we have to remember that this was precisely the conclusion we arrived at, from a consideration of Luigi Groto, Boaistuau, and the Italian novels. The question naturally suggests itself as to whether the source from which Struijs drew was that adaptation of a play or tale

1562, it seems hardly possible to date the unknown source earlier than 1555.

based on, or similar to, Da Porto and Bandello to which we previously referred. It may be thought highly probable that this was so, and we may well believe that there could hardly be two unknown English sources from which Shakspere borrowed; but, although I accept this probability in my chart of the development of the *Romeo* story, there is only inference to support the case.

Lope de Vega's tragi-comedy *Los Castelvines y Monteses*[1] and Don Francisco de Rojas' *Los Bandos de Verona*, both of early date, were based on the version of Bandello. The early German version, *Romeo undh Julietta*, extant probably in 1624, was based on Shakspere's text, of which it is little more than an indifferent remodelling.

The rough draft of a Latin tragedy *Romeus et Julietta* in the British Museum (Sloane MS. 1775, privately printed by Dr. Gollancz) is based on Brooke's poem. It is evidently the author's holograph MS., and as in an adjacent composition in the same hand there is mention of Joseph Barnes the Oxford printer, and *Rex Platonicus*, by Sir Isaac Wake, which itself has a reference to an oration of August, 1605, the Latin text must certainly have been composed early in the 17th Century, and can have no immediate connexion with Shakspere.[2]

---

[1] Both this and the following play were translated by F. W. Cosens and printed privately in 1869. An epitome of Lope de Vega, so translated, is given by Furness in his *Variorum Romeo*, p. 470.

[2] Fuller, p. 43. The MS. contains, besides, a madrigal to the author of *Ignoramus*, acted in 1615.

Early Italian
Play or Novel (?)

Masuccio Salernitano
Cinquante Novelle, 1476

Luigi Da Porto
Giulia e Romeo, c. 1530

Luigi Groto
La Hadriana
1578

Clitia
Giulia e Romeo
1553

Bandello
Giulia e Romeo
1554

Adrian Sevin
*Burglipha and
Halquadrich*
1541-2

Lope de Vega
*Los Castelvines
y Monteses*

F. de Rojas
*Los Bandos
de Verona*

Girolamo della Corte
Storia di Verona
1594

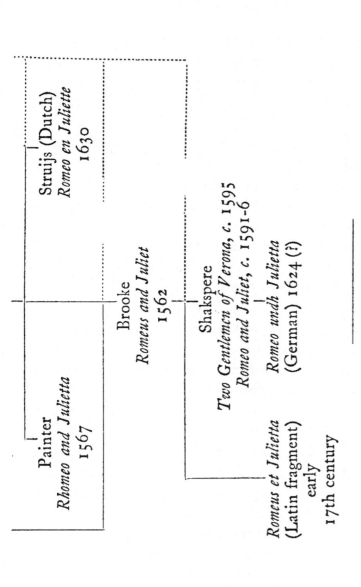

Painter
Rhomeo and Julietta
1567

Struijs (Dutch)
Romeo en Juliette
1630

Brooke
Romeus and Juliet
1562

Shakspere
Two Gentlemen of Verona, c. 1595
Romeo and Juliet, c. 1591-6

Romeo undh Julietta
(German) 1624 (?)

Romeus et Julietta
(Latin fragment)
early
17th century

Connexion which is not certain is signified by dotted lines. Luigi Groto is placed above the 'Earlier English *Play* (?),' etc., for convenience. It should be remembered that the relation of the supposed Early Italian *Play or Novel* to Bandello and Da Porto is not certain. I here consider it as probably another version of the same legend.

INTRODUCTION

Criticism of Brooke's Text.—Different authorities have held the most contrary opinions concerning our author's work. Schlegel says: "There can be nothing more diffuse, more wearisome, than the rhyming history which Shakspere's genius, 'like richest alchemy,' has changed to beauty and to worthiness." Verplanck calls it, with all its faults, a noble poem, and Hudson thinks it has considerable merit. A close criticism of Brooke's poem does not reveal any great powers on the part of its author, and most of the virtues that it has are borrowed.

Brooke's poem, however, is a very able translation of Boaistuau. It renders the sense of its original very faithfully, and in places follows the text with absolute accuracy. So close is Brooke's text to Boaistuau's at times that a perusal of the latter elucidated several words in the English which were otherwise not quite clear.

Brooke's faults are immediately apparent; they are just the faults of a youthful poet of his time. He handles his metre well, but it was little suited to his theme. His poem often displays a good imagination, and possesses delicate sentiment, but contains endless and tiresome repetition of the same ideas and images. Cupid, Fortune, and the three Fates are referred to and apostrophised till one is weary of them. Brooke affected that bombastic and grandiloquent style which was then coming into vogue, and which was characterised by: (*a*) excessive alliteration; (*b*) frequent classical allusions; (*c*) a curious form of " unnatural " natural history, as Collier called it; (*d*) didactic harangues; (*e*) lengthy soliloquies ; (*f*) balanced antithesis ; (*g*) extravagant description and artificial sentiment. Brooke was fond of alliteration, and indulged in it to excess :—

> For delving deeply now in depth of deep despair (l. 1081.)

He often uses half-line rhymes. His speeches are generally tediously prolix and didactic, and some of his soliloquies, dealing with the subtlest and purest emotions and ideas, are expressed at such length, and with such incongruity of metaphor, that they seem to be almost satirical and parodical. Brooke's faults are faults of excess ; and a simile is sometimes so strained and elaborated that the theme itself is quite obscured by it (*see* ll. 1361-78). His style led him to compose lines which are nothing short of ludicrous :—

> "And up unto the heavens she throws her wond'ring head and hands."
> (l. 1928)

He affected archaic word-forms, words, and phrases ; and his nouns are, as a rule, amplified by some heavy and coloured adjective, few of them being able to do duty alone :—

> "With cruel hand my mourning heart would pierce with bloody knife."
> (l. 496)

His characters vacillate with sudden swiftness between violent extremes of emotion ; the passion he portrays strikes one as being, not infinitely tender and delicate, but rude and violent. There is nothing truly organic about the whole poem ; its parts are out of proportion ; it is loose in its construction, and vagarious in its progress. Its atmosphere is that of melodrama, and there is not one truly noble person in it.

But whatever its faults, the reader cannot fail to be struck by a certain grace and aptness for delineation. The poem is consistent in its archaism; and occasion has been found to praise the delicacy of situations in it. One does not expect to find these graces in Brooke. At one point Boaistuau says, "De sorte que s'ils eussent peu commander au ciel comme Josué, etc." (p. 52); Brooke alters this *Josué* to *Alcume:* who was Alcume, and why was the alteration made ?[1]

These and similar considerations led me to believe that Brooke had copied from some older English author, and knowing the resemblance between the Troilus story and Romeo, and noting Brooke's vocabulary, I turned to Chaucer's *Troilus and Criseyde*, and found there at once the poem from which Brooke had borrowed. The full account of Brooke's indebtedness is shown in the Appendix, but the chief points may be summarized here.

Brooke's Debt to Chaucer.—*Troilus,* as the reader will remember, contains the very situations, already worked out, that Brooke had to portray, and the two stories are to a great extent quite parallel: two lovers are secretly betrothed, meet secretly at night in the heroine's house and part at dawning, vacillate between joy and sorrow, are comforted by a mutual friend, are separated by banishment, and have a sad farewell at sunrise after a last night together. This, told by the greatest of our old poets, and accessible at a time

1 *See* Appendix II., l. 824.

when his archaism and others of his characteristics were
becoming the fashionable literary style, was a largesse of
which Brooke was not slow to avail himself.   Most of his
frequent allusions to Fortune and her wheel, to the Fates,
and to Cupid, son of Venus, most of his archaic words, and
some of his proverbial phrases, come from *Troilus*.   Some-
times what was a mere hint in Boaistuau is worked out by
the help of Chaucer.   Juliet, like Criseyde, has golden
locks, and tears them in the same way; Romeus is wise,
like Troilus, has golden locks, too, sorrows the same, and
imagines, like him, that the sun's steeds have gone astray in
the night.   Troilus attending Pandarus' help, and Romeus
attending Laurence's, are both like the patient awaiting the
leech's salve.   Brooke affects, like Chaucer, to be unable to
picture the joy and despair of his characters, and expresses
ignorance as to the sensations of their love, never having ex-
perienced it.   Brooke's sunrises come, in the main, from
Chaucer.

These and many other minor points the reader should find
in Appendix II.   The great question is whether Chaucer
led Brooke to make any additions to the story itself.   We
answer that he did, although these additions are minor ones.
We saw that in the older and now lost English version of
Romeo (probably a play) there was a scene at Laurence's cell,
wherein Romeo laments.   Brooke borrowed this suggestion
from the play, apparently, but developed it from Chaucer,
where there is a similar scene with Troilus.   Troilus not
only laments but becomes furious like a bull; Romeus does

likewise, and the most interesting and remarkable verbal borrowings are to be found at this point. Shakspere did not portray this scene in its entirety, but in his work, too, come out some of these Chaucer phrases obtained through Brooke, and though his scene is apparently based on the lost "original," we learn here that Romeo has been a "madman," and has railed on his birth, etc., as Troilus did in Chaucer and Romeus in Brooke.[1] The second addition made by the help of Chaucer is Romeus' sorrow in his exile, which greatly resembles that of Troilus, and here again we find close verbal borrowings.[2] This was not taken up by Shakspere, and there does not appear to have been any similar incident in the lost "original,"—a consideration which points to the conclusion (borne out by other facts) that Shakspere used Brooke most where his version coincided with the older and unknown source. In determining our author's debt to Chaucer the student should beware of certain remarkable passages in Brooke, often bearing great resemblance to others in Chaucer, but which have come to *Romeus* through Bandello and Boaistuau. In some cases, however, there can be no doubt that such passages, coming through Boaistuau as they did, have yet been moulded into their present form through the influence of similar passages in Chaucer expressing the same idea.[3]

1 *See* the full account, Appendix II., ll. 1287-1507.
2 Appendix II., ll. 1744-72.
3 Appendix II., ll. 208, 314, 457, 824, 891 (?), etc.

Shakspere's Use of Brooke.—It is important to notice how completely the faults which disfigure Brooke's work are absent from that of Shakspere. The intellect of our great poet, always shaping its materials for dramatic purposes, appreciated intuitively that such faults would be fatal to any stage production. Everything artificial had to be discarded; everything adventitious, ornate speeches, etc., had to be put aside. The swift and eager love of Romeo and Juliet, with its natural attributes of changing emotions, had to be presented with all its pure physical and spiritual life and energy. One might say, in comparing the products of each man's labour, that a process of transmutation had taken place; the whole story was changed in the play, given a new impulse, and a deep and lasting significance: in a phrase, Shakspere vitalised Brooke's work.

Romeo is not the earliest play connected with Brooke's poem. All students of Shakspere are aware of the many similarities existing between *The Two Gentlemen of Verona* and *Romeo and Juliet.* It has even been denied that Shakspere was the author of the former play, but the internal evidence which we shall discuss, demonstrates clearly that its author was also the author of *Romeo,* and that he drew much from Brooke's *Romeus.* We have not here the space, and are not required, to detail all the origins ot *The Two Gentlemen*; we shall simply point out the connexion between that play and *Romeo.*

The first point is the connexion between the characters. Many of the characters in *The Two Gentlemen* are earlier sketches of those which find fuller being in *Romeo*. Julia is Juliet in comedy ; Juliet is Julia with all the fresh emotions of youth in play, isolated in an unsympathetic world which is to crush her. Mercutio (Phebidas in Struijs) probably came from the lost source, but one element of his character, his contempt for love, has its counterpart in Valentino, whose talk with the love-sick Proteus recalls the similar scenes between Benvolio and Mercutio and Romeo. Antonio's concern about Proteus is like old Montague's about Romeo, and as Proteus' love turns from Julia to Silvia, so Romeo's turns from Rosaline to Juliet. Valentine's wooing is endangered, like Romeo's relations with Juliet, by her father's desire to wed Silvia to another man ; and Thurio is another county Paris. The old Duke's words to Silvia on her dislike of Thurio are forerunners of Capulet's passionate outburst to Juliet, unwilling to wed Paris. Valentine, like Romeo, was to have ascended to his love's window by means of a rope ladder, but was discovered. Valentine, too, was banished, and was forced to leave his lady ; he went to *Mantua*, and dared not return on pain of death. When asked by the outlaws the cause of his banishment he replied that he had killed a man in honourable fight—an evident reminiscence of the slaying of Tybalt. Proteus' advice to Valentine on his banishment recalls Laurence's to Romeo. Silvia herself planned escape to avoid "a most unholy match," and met her helper at a friar's cell, whereto she had gone ostensibly for the purpose of confession. A Friar Laurence is mentioned in the text.

The second point is the connexion of incidents. Besides the ladder plot, mentioned above, there are several important incidents which merit attention. In Act IV., Scene ii., we find Proteus expressing his affection to Silvia at her window above him. Valentine and Silvia planned secret marriage and flight, and Julia disguised herself in man's attire as Juliet proposed doing.

This evidence is fairly conclusive; but still it might be contended that these points might have been taken from some older and similar play or poem. A consideration of phrases, however, places the matter in a more certain light. This consideration makes the third point. I have not space here to give the quotations. They are printed in Appendices I. and II, where the reader should see lines 207-9, 1145-6, 1209. I omit other phrases, which are somewhat dubious.

We have next to consider *Romeo* itself. That Shakspere used Brooke in the construction of his tragedy is beyond question. His debt is considerable, although it may be that he followed the old source more closely in construction. Brooke himself did not hesitate to depart from his original: he practically created the character of the Nurse; it is in his version first that the names of Capulet's guests are written; he made the apothecary; he developed Romeus' ravings at the cell,—though such a scene, as it occurs in Struijs, must have been in the earlier English source,—and he pictured his sorrow in exile; he introduced the scenes between Romeus and the Nurse, and between the Nurse and Juliet in connexion with arranging the marriage, and created the incident of Romeus giving the money to the Nurse. Of most of these innovations Shakspere availed himself, but his tragedy departs in many important particulars from Brooke's version. These are: (1) the character and death of Mercutio; (2) the compression of the action from over nine months to five days; (3) Tybalt's outcry against Romeo at the feast; (4) the slaying of Tybalt after his killing Mercutio under Romeo's arm, not, as in Brooke, because of a fury like his own, kindled in Romeo; (5) the arrangement between Capulet and Paris to give Juliet to the latter even before her first meeting with Romeo; (6) the slaying of Paris at the tomb; (7) the perfection of the characters. How many of these points are due to Shakspere, and how many to the old source?

Mercutio, we saw, came from the lost "original," but it is probable that Shakspere individualised him more. The compression of the action, a most potent dramatic change, is due to the great dramatist, but the slaying of Mercutio was probably somewhat similar in the lost version; and Paris (as in Struijs) may there have been earlier introduced than in Brooke, but the fore-contract of marriage and the slaying of Paris are Shakespere's own. In the older version, too, there was probably some reference to, or representation of, Tybalt's storm at the feast. The most interesting point, perhaps, is (7) the perfection of the characters. In the poem Romeo and Juliet have both golden hair. Juliet is fourteen years old in the play and sixteen in the poem; the "wily wench," according to Brooke, laughs at deceiving her mother (714),

and following her mother's instructions, she wilfully leads
Paris on to woo her for a number of days, after the banish-
ment of Romeo (2263-75).   How much purer and more
beautiful is Shakspere's heroine !   Brooke's Romeus possesses
none of the refinement and delicacy of Romeo : Romeus is
like a semi-savage in love ; his grief is overdrawn and his
passion is rendered unnatural by Brooke's lengthy rhetoric.
Note how he speaks to Peter in l. 2626.   Laurence, whom
we have come to know as venerable and wise, is yet in the
poem said to have secreted his " fair friends " at his cell in
his youth (1273, and *see* Appendix I., 1267).   The prolixity
of his speeches is quite tiresome : Shakspere's Laurence says
pointedly : "I will be brief" (V. iii. 229), and brief he is,
compared with the Friar in the poem.   For many other
minor points, the use of " Freetown," etc., and the striking
verbal borrowings that Shakspere made from Brooke, the
reader should consult Appendices I. and II.

Shakspere's task, as a dramatist, was to unify and vivify his
narrative, to individualise it and give it an atmosphere in
keeping with its moving love and tragedy.   Every change
that he made was to these ends.   Brooke's story meanders
on like a listless stream in a strange and impossible land ;
Shakspere's sweeps on like a broad and rushing river, singing
and foaming, flashing in sunlight and darkening in cloud,
carrying all things irresistibly to where it plunges over the
precipice into a waste of waters below.   A rapturous passion,
expressed in a perfect lyricism, and reckless of all on earth
that did not lend it glory and add to its greatness, sweeps

through and pervades the play: all the fire and energy of the south is there, the unquestioning idealism of youth which seizes hold of the fairness of the earth, lives in it, and abides by it. Brooke's Romeus can curse the world, can in the extravagant manner of the poem, curse his own life and pray for death; but Romeo never really loses his faith in the things which are, ever possesses his fundamental belief in joy and love. He acts with southern swiftness and resolution, characteristic of a man who revels in all things beautiful and follows unquestioningly the laws of the ages; swiftly he throws aside his love for Rosaline, and swiftly he loves Juliet; swiftly he weds her, and swiftly he leaves her again; when he hears of her supposed death he acts promptly and decisively; no question of the use and fitness of things comes to him; he ponders no action before execution; he troubles about no criterion of certitude or other philosophical problem; he never pauses to consider, like his antithesis Hamlet, the ultimate end of his own life or of another's, or of the fair, warm flesh which he can see and take joy in; and yet, through all, he is no sensualist or materialist, rather one ever alive to the tireless spirit that works in man. If he hesitates, it is his love which holds him; if he complains, it is his love which has caused his trouble; if he weeps, it is not because he believes happiness to be a delusion, but because it is real and good, because he had it once and has it no longer. If we may anywhere profess to see the character of Shakspere in the spring-time of his labours, it must be in the manner he has worked, selected, and developed here.

Previous Editions.—Brooke's poem has often been reprinted. It was first published by Richard Tottel (or Tothill), the great law-printer, in 1562. Only three copies of this edition are known; one in the Malone collection in the Bodleian; another in the library of Mr. Huth; and a third, imperfect, at Trinity College, Cambridge. According to the *Stationers' Registers,* Tottel obtained a license to reprint the book in 1582; no copy of such an edition is known. Ralph Robinson reprinted the original in 1587. Malone printed it again in 1780, and it was reissued in the Shakespeare Variorum Edition of 1821. It appeared in J. P. Collier's *Shakespeare's Library,* 1843. Halliwell reprinted it in his Folio Edition of Shakspere, following Collier; and Hazlitt, correcting his text from the original, printed it once more in his *Shakespeare's Library,* in 1874. The best edition is that by P. A. Daniel, issued by the New Shakspere Society in 1875.

Painter's "Palace of Pleasure."—Painter's *Rhomeo and Julietta* was first published in the second volume of his *Palace of Pleasure,* in 1567. The whole collection of tales was published in two volumes at different dates; of Vol. I. three editions are known, dated respectively 1566, 1569, and 1575; of Vol. II. only two, the first dated November 8th, 1567, while the second, which is dateless, was probably published between 1575 and 1580.[1] The undated edition contains emendations and additions.

[1] Daniel, p. xx.

As Daniel points out, it is probable that Painter occasionally consulted Brooke in making his translation; but his borrowings are neither frequent nor considerable. He takes none of Brooke's innovations, and adheres tenaciously to Boaistuau's text, except where he duplicates terms or misunderstands his original. It is difficult to see in what way Shakspere could have made use of his version. For a fuller discussion of Painter's novel, I refer the reader to Mr. Daniel's Introduction.

Before closing this Introduction I have to express my gratitude to Mr. P. A. Daniel for the kindly and ready permission he gave me to make any use I cared of his edition of Brooke's poem and Painter's novel: of this I availed myself, as the references indicate. To Dr. Furnivall and to Dr. Gollancz I am likewise indebted for kindly help and advice.

THE TRAGICAL HIS-

tory of Romeus and Juliet, writ-

ten first in Italian by Bandell,

and now in English by

Ar. Br.

In ædibus Richardi Tottelli.

Cum Privilegio.

TO THE READER

THE God of all Glory created, universally, all creatures to set forth His praise; both those which we esteem profitable in use and pleasure, and also those which we accompt noisome and loathsome. But principally He hath appointed man the chiefest instrument of His honour, not only for ministering matter thereof in man himself, but as well in gathering out of other the occasions of publishing God's goodness, wisdom, and power. And in like sort, every doing of man hath, by God's dispensation, something whereby God may and ought to be honoured. So the good doings of the good and the evil acts of the wicked, the happy success of the blessed and the woeful proceedings of the miserable, do in divers sort sound one praise of God. And as each flower yieldeth honey to the bee, so every example ministereth good lessons to the well-disposed mind. The glorious triumph of the continent man upon the lusts of wanton flesh, encourageth men to honest restraint of wild affections; the shameful and wretched ends of such as have yielded their liberty thrall to foul desires teach men to withhold themselves from the headlong fall of loose dishonesty. So, to like effect, by sundry means the good man's example biddeth men to be good, and the evil man's mischief warneth men not to be evil. To this good end serve all ill ends of ill beginnings. And to this end, good Reader, is this tragical matter written, to describe unto thee a couple of unfortunate lovers, thralling themselves to unhonest desire ; neglecting the authority and advice of parents and friends; conferring their principal counsels with drunken gossips and superstitious friars (the naturally fit instruments of unchastity) ; attempting all adventures of peril for th' attaining of their wished lust ; using auricular confession, the key of whoredom and treason, for further-ance of their purpose ; abusing the honourable name of lawful marriage to cloak the shame of stolen contracts ; finally by all means of unhonest life hasting to most unhappy death. This precedent, good Reader, shall be to thee, as the slaves of Lacedemon, oppressed with excess of drink, deformed and altered from likeness of men both in mind and use of body, were to the free-born children, so shewed to them by their parents, to th' intent to raise in them an hateful loathing of so filthy beastliness. Here-unto, if you apply it, ye shall deliver my doing from offence and profit yourselves. Though I saw the same argument lately set forth on stage with more commendation than I can look for—being there much better set forth than I have or can do—yet the same matter penned as it is may serve to like good effect, if the readers do bring with them like good minds to consider it, which hath the more encouraged me to publish it, such as it is.

AR. BR.

TO THE READER

AMID the desert rocks, the mountain bear
    Brings forth unformed, unlike herself, her young,
Naught else but lumps of flesh withouten hair:
In tract of time, her often-licking tongue
Gives them such shape as doth, ere long, delight
    The lookers on: Or when one dog doth shake
    With muzzled mouth the joints too weak to fight;
    Or when upright he standeth by his stake,
A noble crest; or wild in savage wood
    A dozen dogs one holdeth at a bay,
    With gaping mouth and stainéd jaws with blood;
    Or else when from the farthest heavens, they
The lode-stars are, the weary pilate's mark,
    In storms to guide to haven the tosséd bark.

        Right so my muse

    Hath now at length, with travail long, brought forth
    Her tender whelps, her divers kinds of style,
    Such as they are, or naught, or little worth,
    Which careful travail and a longer while
May better shape.   The eldest of them, lo!
    I offer to the stake, my youthful work,

Which one reproachful mouth might overthrow:
The rest—unlicked as yet—awhile shall lurk,
Till time give strength to meet and match in fight
With slander's whelps.   Then shall they tell of strife,
Of noble triumphs and deeds of martial might,
And shall give rules of chaste and honest life.
The while I pray that ye with favour blame,
Or rather not reprove the laughing game
                                    Of this my muse.

THE ARGUMENT

LOVE hath inflaméd twain by sudden sight,
  And both do grant the thing that both desire.
They wed in shrift by counsel of a friar.
Young Romeus climbs fair Juliet's bower by night.
Three months he doth enjoy his chief delight.
  By Tybalt's rage provokéd unto ire,
  He payeth death to Tybalt for his hire.
A banished man he 'scapes by secret flight.
New marriage is offered to his wife.
  She drinks a drink that seems to reave her breath:
  They bury her that sleeping yet hath life.
Her husband hears the tidings of her death.
  He drinks his bane.   And she with Romeus' knife,
When she awakes, herself, alas! she slay'th.

ROMEUS AND JULIET

ROMEUS AND JULIET

THERE is beyond the Alps, a town of ancient fame,
  Whose bright renown yet shineth clear : Verona men it
Built in a happy time, built on a fertile soil,   [name ;
Maintainéd by the heavenly fates, and by the townish toil.
The fruitful hills above, the pleasant vales below,   5
The silver stream with channel deep, that thro' the town doth
The store of springs that serve for use, and eke for ease, [flow,
And other more commodities, which profit may and please,—
Eke many certain signs of things betid of old,
To fill the hungry eyes of those that curiously behold, 10
Do make this town to be preferred above the rest
Of Lombard towns, or at the least, comparéd with the best.
In which while Escalus as prince alone did reign,
To reach reward unto the good, to pay the lewd with pain,
Alas, I rue to think, an heavy hap befell :   , 15
Which Boccace scant, not my rude tongue, were able forth to
Within my trembling hand, my pen doth shake for fear, [tell.
And, on my cold amazéd head, upright doth stand my hair.
But sith she doth command, whose hest I must obey,
In mourning verse, a woeful chance to tell I will assay. 20
Help, learnéd Pallas, help, ye Muses with your art,
Help, all ye damnéd fiends to tell of joys returned to smart.

B

Help eke, ye sisters three, my skilless pen t'indite:
For you it caused which I, alas, unable am to write. [place
   There were two ancient stocks, which Fortune high did
Above the rest, indued with wealth, and nobler of their race,
Loved of the common sort, loved of the prince alike,
And like unhappy were they both, when Fortune list to strike;
Whose praise, with equal blast, Fame in her trumpet blew;
The one was clepéd Capulet, and th' other Montague.   30
A wonted use it is, that men of likely sort,
(I wot not by what fury forced) envy each other's port.
So these, whose egall state bred envy pale of hue,   [grew.
And then, of grudging envy's root, black hate and rancour
As, of a little spark, oft riseth mighty fire,   35
So of a kindled spark of grudge, in flames flash out their ire:
And then their deadly food, first hatched of trifling strife,
Did bathe in blood of smarting wounds; it reavéd breath and
No legend lie I tell, scarce yet their eyes be dry,   [life,
That did behold the grisly sight, with wet and weeping
    eye.   40
But when the prudent prince, who there the sceptre held,
So great a new disorder in his commonweal beheld;
By gentle mean he sought, their choler to assuage;
And by persuasion to appease, their blameful furious rage.
But both his words and time, the prince hath spent in vain: 45
So rooted was the inward hate, he lost his busy pain.
When friendly sage advice, ne gentle words avail,
By thund'ring threats, and princely power their courage 'gan
    he quail.

In hope that when he had the wasting flame supprest,
In time he should quite quench the sparks that burned within
    their breast.   50
    Now whilst these kindreds do remain in this estate,
And each with outward friendly show doth hide his inward
One Romeus, who was of race a Montague,   [hate:
Upon whose tender chin, as yet, no manlike beard there grew,
Whose beauty and whose shape so far the rest did stain,   55
That from the chief of Verone youth he greatest fame did gain,
Hath found a maid so fair (he found so foul his hap),
Whose beauty, shape, and comely grace, did so his heart en-
That from his own affairs, his thought she did remove; [trap,
Only he sought to honour her, to serve her and to love. 60
To her he writeth oft, oft messengers are sent,
At length, in hope of better speed, himself the lover went,
Present to plead for grace, which absent was not found ꞉
And to discover to her eye his new receivéd wound.
But she that from her youth was fostered evermore   65
With virtue's food, and taught in school of wisdom's skilful
By answer did cut off th'affections of his love,   [lore;
That he no more occasion had so vain a suit to move.
So stern she was of cheer, for all the pain he took,
That, in reward of toil, she would not give a friendly look. 70
And yet how much she did with constant mind retire;
So much the more his fervent mind was pricked forth by
    desire.
But when he many months, hopeless of his recure,
Had servéd her, who forcéd not what pains he did endure,

At length he thought to leave Verona, and to prove   75
If change of place might change away his ill-bestowéd love;
And speaking to himself, thus 'gan he make his moan:
'What booteth me to love and serve a fell, unthankful one,
Sith that my humble suit and labour sowed in vain,   79
Can reap none other fruit at all but scorn and proud disdain?
What way she seeks to go, the same I seek to run,   [shun.
But she the path wherein I tread, with speedy flight doth
I cannot live, except that near to her I be;
She is aye best content when she is farthest off from me.
Wherefore henceforth I will far from her take my flight; 85
Perhaps mine eye once banishéd by absence from her sight,
This fire of mine, that by her pleasant eyne is fed,
Shall little and little wear away, and quite at last be dead.'
   But whilst he did decree this purpose still to keep,
A contrary, repugnant thought sank in his breast so deep, 90
That doubtful is he now which of the twain is best:
In sighs, in tears, in plaint, in care, in sorrow and unrest,
He moans the day, he wakes the long and weary night; [bright
So deep hath love with piercing hand, y-graved her beauty
Within his breast, and hath so mastered quite his heart, 95
That he of force must yield as thrall;—no way is left to start.
He cannot stay his step, but forth still must he run;
He languisheth and melts away, as snow against the sun.
His kindred and allies do wonder what he ails,
And each of them in friendly wise his heavy hap bewails. 100
But one among the rest, the trustiest of his feres,
Far more than he with counsel filled, and riper of his years,

'Gan sharply him rebuke, such love to him he bare,
That he was fellow of his smart, and partner of his care.
'What mean'st thou, Romeus, quoth he, what doting rage 105
Doth make thee thus consume away the best part of thine age,
In seeking her that scorns, and hides her from thy sight,
Not forcing all thy great expense, ne yet thy honour bright,
Thy tears, thy wretched life, ne thine unspotted truth, 109
Which are of force, I ween, to move the hardest heart to ruth?
Now for our friendship's sake, and for thy health, I pray,
That thou henceforth become thine own.—Oh, give no more
Unto a thankless wight thy precious free estate;   [away
In that thou lovest such a one, thou seem'st thyself to hate.
For she doth love elsewhere,—and then thy time is lorn, 115
Or else (what booteth thee to sue?) Love's court she hath
    forsworn.
Both young thou art of years, and high in Fortune's grace:
What man is better shaped than thou? Who hath a sweeter
    face?
By painful studies' mean, great learning hast thou won; 119
Thy parents have none other heir, thou art their only son.
What greater grief, trowst thou, what woeful deadly smart
Should so be able to distrain thy seely father's heart,
As in his age to see thee plungéd deep in vice,
When greatest hope he hath to hear thy virtue's fame arise?
What shall thy kinsmen think, thou cause of all their ruth? 125
Thy deadly foes do laugh to scorn thy ill-employéd youth.
Wherefore my counsel is, that thou henceforth begin
To know and fly the error which too long thou livedst in.

Remove the veil of love, that keeps thine eyes so blind,
That thou ne canst the ready path of thy forefathers find. 130
But if unto thy will so much in thrall thou art,
Yet in some other place bestow thy witless wand'ring heart.
Choose out some worthy dame, her honour thou and serve,
Who will give ear to thy complaint, and pity ere thou sterve.
But sow no more thy pains in such a barren soil,   135
As yields in harvest time no crop, in recompense of toil.
Ere long the townish dames together will resort;
Some one of beauty, favour, shape, and of so lovely port,
With so fast fixéd eye, perhaps thou mayst behold,   139
That thou shalt quite forget thy love, and passions past of old.'
  The young man's listening ear received the wholesome
    sound,
And reason's truth y-planted so, within his head had ground;
That now with healthy cool y-tempered is the heat,   [fret.
And piecemeal wears away the grief that erst his heart did
To his approved friend a solemn oath he plight,   145
At every feast y-kept by day, and banquet made by night,
At pardons in the church, at games in open street,
And everywhere he would resort where ladies wont to meet;
Eke should his savage heart like all indifferently,
For he would view and judge them all with unalluréd eye. 150
How happy had he been, had he not been forsworn;
But twice as happy had he been, had he been never born.
For ere the moon could thrice her wasted horns renew,
False Fortune cast for him, poor wretch, a mischief new to
    brew.

The weary winter nights restore the Christmas games, 155
And now the season doth invite to banquet townish dames.
And first in Capel's house, the chief of all the kin
Spar'th for no cost, the wonted use of banquets to begin.
No lady fair or foul was in Verona town,
No knight or gentleman of high or low renown, 160
But Capulet himself hath bid unto his feast,
Or by his name in paper sent, appointed as a geast.
Young damsels thither flock, of bachelors a rout,
Not so much for the banquet's sake, as beauties to search out.
But not a Montague would enter at his gate, 165
(For as you heard, the Capulets and they were at debate)
Save Romeus, and he, in mask with hidden face,
The supper done, with other five did press into the place.
When they had masked awhile, with dames in courtly wise,
All did unmask, the rest did show them to their ladies' eyes;
But bashful Romeus with shamefast face forsook 171
The open press, and him withdrew into the chamber's nook.
But brighter than the sun, the waxen torches shone,
That maugre what he could, he was espied of everyone.
But of the women chief, their gazing eyes that threw, 175
To wonder at his sightly shape and beauty's spotless hue,
With which the heavens him had and nature so bedecked,
That ladies thought the fairest dames were foul in his respect.
And in their head beside, another wonder rose,
How he durst put himself in throng among so many foes. 180
Of courage stout they thought his coming to proceed:
And women love an hardy heart, as I in stories read.

The Capulets disdain the presence of their foe,
Yet they suppress their stirréd ire, the cause I do not know:
Perhaps t' offend their guests the courteous knights are loth, 185
Perhaps they stay from sharp revenge, dreading the Prince's
Perhaps for that they shamed to exercise their rage   [wroth.
Within their house, 'gainst one alone, and him of tender age.
They use no taunting talk, ne harm him by their deed;
They neither say, 'What mak'st thou here?' ne yet they say,
        'God speed.'   190
So that he freely might the ladies view at ease;
And they also beholding him, their change of fancies please;
Which Nature had him taught to do with such a grace,
That there was none but joyéd at his being there in place.
With upright beam he weighed the beauty of each dame, 195
And judged who best, and who next her, was wrought in
        Nature's frame.
At length he saw a maid, right fair, of perfect shape,
Which Theseus or Paris would have chosen to their rape.
Whom erst he never saw; of all she pleased him most;
Within himself he said to her, Thou justly may'st thee boast 200
Of perfect shape's renown, and beauty's sounding praise,
Whose like ne hath, ne shall be seen, ne liveth in our days.
And whilst he fixed on her his partial piercéd eye,
His former love, for which of late he ready was to die,
Is now as quite forgot, as it had never been: 205
The proverb saith, 'Unminded oft are they that are unseen.'
And as out of a plank a nail a nail doth drive,
So novel love out of the mind the ancient love doth rive.

This sudden kindléd fire in time is wox so great, [fiery heat.
That only death and both their bloods might quench the
When Romeus saw himself in this new tempest tossed, 211
Where both was hope of pleasant port, and danger to be lost,
He doubtful, scarcely knew what countenance to keep;
In Lethe's flood his wonted flames were quenched and
    drenchéd deep.
Yea, he forgets himself, ne is the wretch so bold 215
To ask her name, that without force hath him in bondage
Ne how t' unloose his bonds doth the poor fool devise, [fold.
But only seeketh by her sight to feed his hungry eyes: [bait:
Through them he swalloweth down love's sweet impoisoned
How surely are the wareless wrapt by those that lie in wait!
So is the poison spread throughout his bones and veins, 221
That in a while, alas, the while, it hasteth deadly pains.
Whilst Juliet, for so this gentle damsel hight,
From side to side on every one did cast about her sight:
At last her floating eyes were anchored fast on him, 225
Who for her sake did banish health and freedom from each
He in her sight did seem to pass the rest as far [limb.
As Phœbus' shining beams do pass the brightness of a star.
In wait lay warlike Love with golden bow and shaft,
And to his ear with steady hand the bowstring up he raft.
Till now she had escaped his sharp inflaming dart, 231
Till now he listed not assault her young and tender heart.
His whetted arrow loosed, so touched her to the quick,
That through the eye it strake the heart, and there the
    head did stick.

It booted not to strive, for why, she wanted strength; 235
The weaker aye unto the strong of force must yield, at length.
The pomps now of the feast her heart 'gins to despise;
And only joyeth when her eyne meet with her lover's eyes.
When their new smitten hearts had fed on loving gleams,
Whilst, passing to and fro their eyes, y-mingled were their
      beams.
Each of these lovers 'gan by other's looks to know,
That friendship in their breast had root, and both would
      have it grow.   242
When thus in both their hearts had Cupid made his breach,
And each of them had sought the mean to end the war by
Dame Fortune did assent their purpose to advance,   [speech,
With torch in hand a comely knight did fetch her forth to
She quit herself so well, and with so trim a grace,   [dance;
That she the chief praise won that night from all Verona race.
The whilst our Romeus a place had warely won,   249
Nigh to the seat where she must sit, the dance once being
Fair Juliet turnéd to her chair with pleasant cheer, [done.
And glad she was her Romeus approachéd was so near.
At th' one side of her chair her lover Romeo,
And on the other side there sat one called Mercutio;
A courtier that each where was highly had in price,   255
For he was courteous of his speech, and pleasant of device.
Even as a lion would among the lambs be bold,
Such was among the bashful maids Mercutio to behold.
With friendly gripe he seized fair Juliet's snowish hand:
A gift he had that Nature gave him in his swathing band,

That frozen mountain ice was never half so cold,   261
As were his hands, though ne'er so near the fire he did them
As soon as had the knight the virgin's right hand raught, [hold.
Within his trembling hand her left hath loving Romeus
For he wist well himself for her abode most pain,   [caught.
And well he wist she loved him best, unless she list to feign.
Then she with tender hand his tender palm hath pressed ;
What joy, trow you, was grafféd so in Romeus' cloven breast ?
The sudden sweet delight hath stoppéd quite his tongue,
Ne can he claim of her his right, ne crave redress of wrong.
But she espied straightway, by changing of his hue   271
From pale to red, from red to pale, and so from pale anew,
That veh'ment love was cause, why so his tongue did stay,
And so much more she longed to hear what Love could
        teach him say.
When she had longéd long, and he long held his peace,   275
And her desire of hearing him, by silence did increase,
At last, with trembling voice and shamefast cheer, the maid
Unto her Romeus turned herself, and thus to him she said :
    ' O blessed be the time of thy arrival here : '   [near,
But ere she could speak forth the rest, to her Love drew so
And so within her mouth, her tongue he gluéd fast,   281
That no one word could 'scape her more than what already
        passed.   ⟅
In great contented ease the young man straight is rapt :
' What chance,' quoth he, ' un'ware to me, O lady mine, is hapt,
That gives you worthy cause my coming here to bliss ? '   285
Fair Juliet was come again unto herself by this :

First ruthfully she looked, then said with smiling cheer:
'Marvel no whit, my heart's delight, my only knight and fere,
Mercutio's icy hand had all-to frozen mine,
And of thy goodness thou again hast warméd it with thine.'
Whereto with stayéd brow, 'gan Romeus to reply: 291
'If so the gods have granted me such favour from the sky,
That by my being here some service I have done
That pleaseth you, I am as glad, as I a realm had won. 294
O well-bestowéd time, that hath the happy hire,   [desire.
Which I would wish, if I might have, my wishéd heart's
For I of God would crave, as price of pains forepast,
To serve, obey, and honour you, so long as life shall last;
As proof shall teach you plain, if that you like to try
His faultless truth, that nill for aught unto his lady lie.   300
But if my touchéd hand have warméd yours some deal,
Assure yourself the heat is cold, which in your hand you feel,
Compared to such quick sparks and glowing furious glead,
As from your beauty's pleasant eyne, Love causéd to proceed;
Which have so set on fire each feeling part of mine,   305
That lo, my mind doth melt away, my outward parts do pine.
And but you help, all whole, to ashes shall I turn;
Wherefore, alas, have ruth on him, whom you do force to
      burn.'
   Even with his ended tale, the torches' dance had end,
And Juliet of force must part from her new chosen friend.
His hand she claspéd hard, and all her parts did shake, 311
When leisureless with whisp'ring voice thus did she answer
      make :

You are no more your own, dear friend, than I am yours,
My honour savéd, prest t'obey your will, while life en-
    dures.
Lo, here the lucky lot that seld true lovers find,
Each takes away the other's heart, and leaves the own behind.
A happy life is love, if God grant from above,   317
That heart with heart by even weight do make exchange of
But Romeus gone from her, his heart for care is cold ;   [love.
He hath forgot to ask her name that hath his heart in hold.
With forgéd careless cheer, of one he seeks to know,   321
Both how she hight, and whence she came, that him enchanted
So hath he learned her name, and know'th she is no geast, [so.
Her father was a Capulet, and master of the feast.
Thus hath his foe in choice to give him life or death,   325
That scarcely can his woeful breast keep in the lively breath.
Wherefore with piteous plaint fierce Fortune doth he blame,
That in his ruth and wretched plight doth seek her laugh-
And he reproveth Love, chief cause of his unrest, [ing game.
Who ease and freedom hath exiled out of his youthful breast.
Twice hath he made him serve, hopeless of his reward ; 331
Of both the ills to choose the less, I ween the choice were
First to a ruthless one he made him sue for grace,   [hard.
And now with spur he forceth him to run an endless race.
Amid these stormy seas one anchor doth him hold,   335
He serveth not a cruel one, as he had done of old.
And therefore is content, and chooseth still to serve,
Though hap should swear that guerdonless the wretched
    wight should sterve.

The lot of Tantalus is, Romeus, like to thine;
For want of food amid his food, the miser still doth pine.
    As careful was the maid what way were best devise   341
To learn his name, that entertained her in so gentle wise,
Of whom her heart received so deep, so wide a wound.
An ancient dame she called to her, and in her ear 'gan round.
This old dame in her youth had nursed her with her milk,
With slender needle taught her sew, and how to spin with silk.
'What twain are those,' quoth she, 'which press unto the door,
Whose pages in their hand do bear two torches light before?'
And then as each of them had of his household name,
So she him named yet once again, the young and wily dame.
'And tell me, who is he with visor in his hand,   351
That yonder doth in masking weed beside the window stand?'
'His name is Romeus,' said she, 'a Montague, [households rue.'
Whose father's pride first stirred the strife which both your
The word of Montague her joys did overthrow,   355
And straight instead of happy hope, despair began to grow.
'What hap have I,' quoth she, 'to love my father's foe?
What, am I weary of my weal? What, do I wish my woe?'
But though her grievous pains distrained her tender heart,
Yet with an outward show of joy she cloakéd inward smart;
And of the courtlike dames her leave so courtly took,   361
That none did guess the sudden change by changing of her
Then at her mother's hest to chamber she her hied,   [look.
So well she feigned, mother ne nurse the hidden harm descried.
But when she should have slept, as wont she was, in bed, 365
Not half a wink of quiet sleep could harbour in her head.

For lo, an hugy heap of divers thoughts arise,   [her eyes.
That rest have banished from her heart, and slumber from
And now from side to side she tosseth and she turns,
And now for fear she shivereth, and now for love she burns.
And now she likes her choice, and now her choice she blames,
And now each hour within her head a thousand fancies frames.
Sometime in mind to stop amid her course begun,   373
Sometime she vows, what so betide, th' attempted race to run.
Thus danger's dread and love within the maiden fought :
The fight was fierce, continuing long by their contrary
In turning maze of love she wand'reth to and fro, [thought.
Then standeth doubtful what to do, lost, overpressed with woe.
How so her fancies cease, her tears did never blin, [begin :
With heavy cheer and wrangéd hands thus doth her plaint
    'Ah, silly fool,' quoth she, 'y-caught in subtle snare! [care]
Ah, wretchéd wench, bewrapt in woe !   Ah, caitiff clad with
Whence come these wand'ring thoughts to thy unconstant
    breast ?
By straying thus from reason's law, that reave thy wonted rest.
What if his subtle brain to feign have taught his tongue, 385
And so the snake that lurks in grass thy tender heart hath
What if with friendly speech the traitor lie in wait, [stung ?
As oft the poisoned hook is hid, wrapt in the pleasant bait ?
Oft under cloak of truth hath Falsehood served her lust ;
And turned their honour into shame, that did so slightly
What, was not Dido so, a crownéd queen, defamed ? [trust.
And eke, for such a heinous crime, have men not Theseus
    blamed ?

A thousand stories more, to teach me to beware,
In Boccace and in Ovid's books too plainly written are.
Perhaps, the great revenge he cannot work by strength, 395
By subtle sleight, my honour stained, he hopes to work at
So shall I seek to find my father's foe his game;   [length.
So, I befiled, Report shall take her trump of black defame,
Whence she with puffèd cheek shall blow a blast so shrill
Of my dispraise, that with the noise Verona shall she fill. 400
Then I, a laughing-stock through all the town become,
Shall hide myself, but not my shame, within an hollow
Straight underneath her foot she treadeth in the dust [tomb.
Her troublesome thought, as wholly vain, y-bred of fond
No, no, by God above, I wot it well, quoth she, [distrust.
Although I rashly spake before, in no wise can it be   406
That where such perfect shape with pleasant beauty rests,
There crooked craft and treason black should be appointed
Sage writers say, the thoughts are dwelling in the eyne; [guests.
Then sure I am, as Cupid reigns, that Romeus is mine. 410
The tongue the messenger eke call they of the mind;
So that I see he loveth me; shall I then be unkind?
His face's rosy hue I saw full oft to seek;   [cheek.
And straight again it flashèd forth, and spread in either
His fixèd heavenly eyne, that through me quite did pierce
His thoughts unto my heart, my thought they seemèd to re-
What meant his falt'ring tongue in telling of his tale? [hearse.
The trembling of his joints, and eke his colour waxen pale?
And whilst I talked with him, himself he hath exiled
Out of himself, as seemèd me, ne was I sure beguiled. 420

Those arguments of love Craft wrate not in his face,
But Nature's hand, when all deceit was banished out of place.
What other certain signs seek I of his good will?   [still,
These do suffice; and steadfast I will love and serve him
Till Atropos shall cut my fatal thread of life,   425
So that he mind to make of me his lawful wedded wife.
For so perchance this new alliance may procure
Unto our houses such a peace as ever shall endure.'
    Oh, how we can persuade ourself to what we like,   429
And how we can dissuade our mind, if aught our mind mis-
Weak arguments are strong, our fancies straight to frame [like!
To pleasing things, and eke to shun if we mislike the same.
The maid had scarcely yet ended the weary war,   [star
Kept in her heart by striving thoughts, when every shining
Had paid his borrowed light, and Phœbus spread in skies 435
His golden rays, which seemed to say, now time it is to rise.
And Romeus had by this forsaken his weary bed,   [head.
Where restless he a thousand thoughts had forgéd in his
And while with ling'ring step by Juliet's house he passed,
And upwards to her windows high his greedy eyes did cast,
His love that looked for him there 'gan he straight espy. 441
With pleasant cheer each greeted is; she followeth with her
His parting steps, and he oft looketh back again,   [eye
But not so oft as he desires; warely he doth refrain.
What life were like to love, if dread of jeopardy   445
Y-souréd not the sweet, if love were free from jealousy!
But she more sure within, unseen of any wight,
When so he comes, looks after him till he be out of sight.

In often passing so, his busy eyes he threw,
That every pane and tooting hole the wily lover knew. 450
In happy hour he doth a garden plot espy,   [descry;
From which, except he warely walk, men may his love
For lo, it fronted full upon her leaning place,   [face.
Where she is wont to show her heart by cheerful friendly
And lest the arbours might their secret love bewray,   455
He doth keep back his forward foot from passing there by day;
But when on earth the Night her mantle black hath spread;
Well armed he walketh forth alone, ne dreadful foes doth dread.
Whom maketh Love not bold, nay, whom makes he not blind?
He reaveth danger's dread oft-times out of the lover's mind.
By night he passeth here, a week or two in vain;   461
And for the missing of his mark his grief hath him nigh
And Juliet that now doth lack her heart's relief,   [slain.
Her Romeus' pleasant eyne, I mean, is almost dead for grief.
Each day she changeth hours (for lovers keep an hour 465
When they are sure to see their love in passing by their
Impatient of her woe, she happed to lean one night [bower).
Within her window, and anon the moon did shine so bright
That she espied her love: her heart revivéd sprang; [wrang.
And now for joy she claps her hands, which erst for woe she
Eke Romeus, when he saw his long desiréd sight,   471
His mourning cloak of moan cast off, hath clad him with
Yet dare I say, of both that she rejoicéd more: [delight.
His care was great, hers twice as great was all the time before;
For whilst she knew not why he did himself absent, [lament.
Aye doubting both his health and life, his death she did

For love is fearful oft where is no cause of fear,   [were.
And what love fears, that love laments, as though it chancéd
Of greater cause alway is greater work y-bred;   [be dead.
While he nought doubteth of her health, she dreads lest he
When only absence is the cause of Romeus' smart,   481
By happy hope of sight again he feeds his fainting heart.
What wonder then if he were wrapped in less annoy?
What marvel if by sudden sight she fed of greater joy?
His smaller grief or joy no smaller love do prove;   485
Ne, for she passéd him in both, did she him pass in love:
But each of them alike did burn in equal flame,
The well-beloving knight and eke the well-belovéd dame.
Now whilst with bitter tears her eyes as fountains run,
With whispering voice, y-broke with sobs, thus is her tale
   O Romeus, of your life too lavas sure you are,   [begun:
That in this place, and at this time, to hazard it you dare.
What if your deadly foes, my kinsmen, saw you here? 493
Like lions wild, your tender parts asunder would they tear.
In ruth and in disdain, I, weary of my life,   [bloody knife.
With cruel hand my mourning heart would pierce with
For you, mine own, once dead, what joy should I have here?
And eke my honour stained, which I than life do hold more
   'Fair lady mine, dame Juliet, my life,' quod he,   [dear.
'Even from my birth committed was to fatal sisters three. 500
They may in spite of foes draw forth my lively thread;
And they also, whoso saith nay, asunder may it shred.
But who to reave my life, his rage and force would bend,
Perhaps should try unto his pain how I it could defend.

Ne yet I love it so, but always for your sake,　　　505
A sacrifice to death I would my wounded corpse betake.
If my mishap were such, that here before your sight,
I should restore again to death, of life, my borrowed light,
This one thing and no more my parting sprite would rue,
That part he should before that you by certain trial knew
The love I owe to you, the thrall I languish in,　　　511
And how I dread to lose the gain which I do hope to win;
And how I wish for life, not for my proper ease,
But that in it you might I love, you honour, serve and please,
Till deadly pangs the sprite out of the corpse shall send:'　515
And thereupon he sware an oath, and so his tale had end.

　　Now love and pity boil in Juliet's ruthful breast;
In window on her leaning arm her weary head doth rest;
Her bosom bathed in tears, to witness inward pain,
With dreary cheer to Romeus thus answered she again:　520
　'Ah, my dear Romeus, keep in these words,' quod she,
'For lo, the thought of such mischance already maketh me
For pity and for dread well-nigh to yield up breath;
In even balance peiséd are my life and eke my death.
For so my heart is knit, yea, made one self with yours,　525
That sure there is no grief so small, by which your mind
But as you suffer pain, so I do bear in part,　　　[endures,
Although it lessens not your grief, the half of all your smart.
But these things overpast, if of your health and mine
You have respect, or pity aught my teary, weeping eyne,
In few unfainéd words your hidden mind unfold,　　　531
That as I see your pleasant face, your heart I may behold.

For if you do intend my honour to defile,
In error shall you wander still, as you have done this while ;
But if your thought be chaste, and have on virtue ground,
If wedlock be the end and mark which your desire hath found,
Obedience set aside, unto my parents due,   537
The quarrel eke that long ago between our households grew,
Both me and mine I will all whole to you betake,
And following you whereso you go, my father's house forsake.
But if by wanton love and by unlawful suit   541
You think in ripest years to pluck my maidenhood's dainty
You are beguiled ; and now your Juliet you beseeks [fruit,
To cease your suit, and suffer her to live among her likes.'
   Then Romeus, whose thought was free from foul desire,
And to the top of virtue's height did worthily aspire,   546
Was filled with greater joy than can my pen express, [guess.
Or, till they have enjoyed the like, the hearer's heart can
And then with joinéd hands, heaved up into the skies,
He thanks the Gods, and from the heavens for vengeance down
If he have other thought but as his lady spake ;   [he cries,
And then his look he turned to her, and thus did answer
   ' Since, lady, that you like to honour me so much [make :
As to accept me for your spouse, I yield myself for such.
In true witness whereof, because I must depart,   555
Till that my deed do prove my word, I leave in pawn my
To-morrow eke betimes before the sun arise,   [heart.
To Friar Laurence will I wend, to learn his sage advice.
He is my ghostly sire, and oft he hath me taught   [sought.
What I should do in things of weight, when I his aid have

And at this self-same hour, I plight you here my faith,   561
I will be here, if you think good, to tell you what he saith.'
She was contented well; else favour found he none
That night at lady Juliet's hand, save pleasant words alone.

   This barefoot friar girt with cord his grayish weed,   565
For he of Francis' order was, a friar, as I rede.
Not as the most was he, a gross unlearnéd fool,
But doctor of divinity proceeded he in school.
The secrets eke he knew in Nature's works that lurk;   [work.
By magic's art most men supposed that he could wonders
Ne doth it ill beseem divines those skills to know,   571
If on no harmful deed they do such skilfulness bestow;
For justly of no art can men condemn the use,
But right and reason's lore cry out against the lewd abuse.
The bounty of the friar and wisdom hath so won   [run,
The townsfolks' hearts, that well nigh all to Friar Laurence
To shrive themself; the old, the young, the great and small;
Of all he is belovéd well, and honoured much of all.   578
And, for he did the rest in wisdom far exceed,   [need.
The prince by him, his counsel craved, was holp at time of
Betwixt the Capulets and him great friendship grew,   581
A secret and assuréd friend unto the Montague.
Loved of this young man more than any other guest,
The friar eke of Verone youth aye likéd Romeus best;
For whom he ever hath in time of his distress,   585
As erst you heard, by skilful lore found out his harm's re-
— To him is Romeus gone, ne stay'th he till the morrow;   [dress.
To him he painteth all his case, his passéd joy and sorrow.

How he hath her espied with other dames in dance,
And how that first to talk with her himself he did advance;
Their talk and change of looks he 'gan to him declare, 591
And how so fast by faith and troth they both y-coupléd are,
That neither hope of life, nor dread of cruel death, [breath.
Shall make him false his faith to her, while life shall lend him
And then with weeping eyes he prays his ghostly sire 595
To further and accomplish all their honest hearts' desire.
A thousand doubts and mo in th' old man's head arose,
A thousand dangers like to come the old man doth disclose,
And from the spousal rites he redeth him refrain,
Perhaps he shall be bet advised within a week or twain.
Advice is banished quite from those that follow love, 601
Except advice to what they like their bending mind do move.
As well the father might have counselled him to stay [way,
That from a mountain's top thrown down is falling half the
As warn his friend to stop amid his race begun, 605
Whom Cupid with his smarting whip enforceth forth to run.
Part won by earnest suit, the friar doth grant at last;
And part, because he thinks the storms, so lately overpast,
Of both the households' wrath, this marriage might appease;
So that they should not rage again, but quite for ever cease.
The respite of a day he asketh to devise 611
What way were best, unknown, to end so great an enterprise.
The wounded man that now doth deadly pains endure,
Scarce patient tarrieth whilst his leech doth make the salve
— So Romeus hardly grants a short day and a night, [to cure:
Yet needs he must, else must he want his only heart's delight.

You see that Romeus no time or pain doth spare;   617
Think that the whilst fair Juliet is not devoid of care.
Young Romeus poureth forth his hap and his mishap
Into the friar's breast; but where shall Juliet unwrap   620
The secrets of her heart?   To whom shall she unfold
Her hidden burning love, and eke her thought and cares so
The nurse of whom I spake, within her chamber lay, [cold?
Upon the maid she waiteth still; to her she doth bewray
Her new receivéd wound, and then her aid doth crave, 625
In her, she saith, it lies to spill, in her, her life to save.
Not easily she made the froward nurse to bow,   [vow
But won at length with promised hire, she made a solemn
To do what she commands, as handmaid of her hest;
Her mistress' secrets hide she will within her covert breast.
    To Romeus she goes; of him she doth desire   631
To know the mean of marriage, by counsel of the friar.
'On Saturday,' quod he, 'if Juliet come to shrift,   [drift?'
She shall be shrived and marriéd; how like you, nurse, this
'Now by my truth,' quod she, 'God's blessing have your heart,
For yet in all my life I have not heard of such a part. 636
Lord, how you young men can such crafty wiles devise,
If that you love the daughter well, to blear the mother's eyes.
An easy thing it is with cloak of holiness
To mock the seely mother, that suspecteth nothing less. 640
But that it pleaséd you to tell me of the case,
For all my many years, perhaps, I should have found it scarce.
Now for the rest let me and Juliet alone;
To get her leave, some feat excuse I will devise anon;

For that her golden locks by sloth have been unkempt, 645
Or for unwares some wanton dream the youthful damsel
Or for in thoughts of love her idle time she spent, [drempt,
Or otherwise within her heart deservéd to be shent.
I know her mother will in no case say her nay;
I warrant you, she shall not fail to come on Saturday.' 650
And then she swears to him, the mother loves her well;
And how she gave her suck in youth, she leaveth not to tell.
'A pretty babe,' quod she, 'it was when it was young;
Lord, how it could full prettily have prated with it tongue!
A thousand times and more I laid her on my lap, 655
And clapped her on the buttock soft, and kissed where I did
And gladder then was I of such a kiss, forsooth, [clap.
Than I had been to have a kiss of some old lecher's mouth.'
And thus of Juliet's youth began this prating nurse,
And of her present state to make a tedious, long discourse.
For though he pleasure took in hearing of his love, 661
The message' answer seeméd him to be of more behove.
But when these beldames sit at ease upon their tail,
The day and eke the candle-light before their talk shall fail.
And part they say is true, and part they do devise, 665
Yet boldly do they chat of both, when no man checks their
Then he six crowns of gold out of his pocket drew, [lies.
And gave them her; 'A slight reward,' quod he, 'and so, adieu.'
In seven years twice told she had not bowed so low [bestow
Her crooked knees, as now they bow; she swears she will
Her crafty wit, her time, and all her busy pain, 671
To help him to his hopéd bliss; and, cow'ring down again,

She takes her leave, and home she hies with speedy pace;
The chamber door she shuts, and then she saith with smiling
'Good news for thee, my girl, good tidings I thee bring. [face:
Leave off thy wonted song of care, and now of pleasure sing.
For thou may'st hold thyself the happiest under sun,   677
That in so little while, so well, so worthy a knight hast won.
The best y-shaped is he, and hath the fairest face   [grace:
Of all this town, and there is none hath half so good a
So gentle of his speech, and of his counsel wise:'   681
And still with many praises more she heaved him to the skies.
'Tell me else what,' quod she, 'this evermore I thought;
But of our marriage, say at once, what answer have you brought?'
'Nay, soft,' quoth she, 'I fear your hurt by sudden joy.'   685
'I list not play,' quod Juliet, 'although thou list to toy.'
How glad, trow you, was she, when she had heard her say,
No farther off than Saturday deferréd was the day!
Again the ancient nurse doth speak of Romeus,   [thus.'
'And then,' said she, 'he spake to me, and then I spake him
Nothing was done or said that she hath left untold,   691
Save only one, that she forgot, the taking of the gold.
'There is no loss,' quod she, 'sweet wench, to loss of time,
Ne in thine age shalt thou repent so much of any crime.
For when I call to mind my former passéd youth,   695
One thing there is which most of all doth cause my endless
At sixteen years I first did choose my loving fere,   [ruth.
And I was fully ripe before, I dare well say, a year.
The pleasure that I lost, that year so overpast,   [last.
A thousand times I have bewept, and shall while life doth

In faith it were a shame,—yea, sin it were, y-wis,   701
When thou may'st live in happy joy, to set light by thy bliss.'
She that this morning could her mistress' mind dissuade,
Is now become an oratress, her lady to persuade.
If any man be here whom love hath clad with care,   705
To him I speak; if thou wilt speed, thy purse thou must not
Two sorts of men there are, seld welcome in at door, [spare,
The wealthy sparing niggard, and the suitor that is poor.
For glitt'ring gold is wont by kind to move the heart;
And oftentimes a slight reward doth cause a more desart.
Y-written have I read, I wot not in what book,   711
There is no better way to fish than with a golden hook.
Of Romeus these two do sit and chat awhile,   [beguile.
And to themself they laugh how they the mother shall
A feat excuse they find, but sure I know it not,   715
And leave for her to go to shrift on Saturday she got.
So well this Juliet, this wily wench did know
Her mother's angry hours, and eke the true bent of her bow.
The Saturday betimes, in sober weed y-clad,   [sad.
She took her leave, and forth she went with visage grave and
With her the nurse is sent, as bridle of her lust,   721
With her the mother sends a maid almost of equal trust.
Betwixt her teeth the bit the jennet now hath caught,
So warely eke the virgin walks, her maid perceiveth nought.
She gazeth not in church on young men of the town,   725
Ne wand'reth she from place to place, but straight she kneeleth
Upon an altar's step, where she devoutly prays,   [down
And there upon her tender knees the weary lady stays;

Whilst she doth send her maid the certain truth to know,
If Friar Laurence leisure had to hear her shrift, or no. 730
Out of his shriving place he comes with pleasant cheer; [near.
The shamefast maid with bashful brow to himward draweth
'Some great offence,' quoth he, 'you have committed late,
Perhaps you have displeased your friend by giving him a
Then turning to the nurse and to the other maid, [mate.'
'Go, hear a mass or two,' quod he, 'which straightway shall
For, her confession heard, I will unto you twain [be said.
The charge that I received of you restore to you again.'
What, was not Juliet, trow you, right well apaid? 739
That for this trusty friar hath changed her young mistrusting
I dare well say, there is in all Verona none, [maid?
But Romeus, with whom she would so gladly be alone.
Thus to the friar's cell they both forth walkéd bin;
He shuts the door as soon as he and Juliet were in.
But Romeus, her friend, was entered in before, 745
And there had waited for his love, two hours large and more.
Each minute seemed an hour, and every hour a day,
'Twixt hope he livéd and despair of coming or of stay.
Now wavering hope and fear are quite fled out of sight,
For what he hoped he hath at hand, his pleasant, chief delight.
And joyful Juliet is healed of all her smart, 751
For now the rest of all her parts have found her straying heart.
Both their confessions first the friar hath heard them make.
And then to her with louder voice thus Friar Laurence spake:
    'Fair lady Juliet, my ghostly daughter dear, 755
As far as I of Romeus learn, who by you standeth here,

'Twixt you it is agreed, that you shall be his wife,
And he your spouse in steady truth, till death shall end your
Are you both fully bent to keep this great behest?'   [life.
And both the lovers said, it was their only heart's request.
When he did see their minds in links of love so fast,   761
When in the praise of wedlock's state some skilful talk was
When he had told at length the wife what was her due, [past,
His duty eke by ghostly talk the youthful husband knew;
How that the wife in love must honour and obey,   765
What love and honour he doth owe, and debt that he must
The words pronouncéd were which holy church of old [pay.
Appointed hath for marriage, and she a ring of gold
Received of Romeus; and then they both arose.   [disclose,
To whom the friar then said: 'Perchance apart you will
Betwixt yourself alone, the bottom of your heart;   771
Say on at once, for time it is that hence you should depart.'
Then Romeus said to her, both loth to part so soon,
'Fair lady, send to me again your nurse this afternoon.
Of cord I will bespeak a ladder by that time;   775
By which, this night, while others sleep, I will your window
Then will we talk of love and of our old despairs,   [climb.
And then, with longer leisure had, dispose our great affairs.'

These said, they kiss, and then part to their fathers' house,
The joyful bride unto her home, to his eke go'th the spouse:
Contented both, and yet both uncontented still,   781
Till Night and Venus' child give leave the wedding to fulfil.
The painful soldier, sore y-beat with weary war,   [far,
The merchant eke that needful things doth dread to fetch from

The ploughman that for doubt of fierce invading foes, 785
Rather to sit in idle ease than sow his tilt hath chose,
Rejoice to hear proclaimed the tidings of the peace ; [cease,
Not pleasured with the sound so much ; but, when the wars do
Then ceaséd are the harms which cruel war brings forth :
The merchant then may boldly fetch his wares of precious
Dreadless the husbandman doth till his fertile field. [worth ;
For wealth, her mate, not for herself, is peace so precious
So lovers live in care, in dread, and in unrest,   [held :
And deadly war by striving thoughts they keep within their
But wedlock is the peace whereby is freedom won [breast :
To do a thousand pleasant things that should not else be done.
The news of ended war these two have heard with joy, 797
But now they long the fruit of peace with pleasure to enjoy.
In stormy wind and wave, in danger to be lost,
Thy steerless ship, O Romeus, hath been long while betossed ;
The seas are now appeased, and thou, by happy star,   801
Art come in sight of quiet haven ; and, now the wrackful
Is hid with swelling tide, boldly thou may'st resort   [bar
Unto thy wedded lady's bed, thy long desiréd port.
God grant, no folly's mist so dim thy inward sight,   805
That thou do miss the channel that doth lead to thy delight.
God grant, no danger's rock, y-lurking in the dark,
Before thou win the happy port, wrack thy sea-beaten bark.
A servant Romeus had, of word and deed so just,   [trust.
That with his life, if need required, his master would him
His faithfulness had oft our Romeus proved of old ;   811
And therefore all that yet was done unto his man he told,

Who straight, as he was charged, a corden ladder looks,
To which he hath made fast two strong and crooked iron
The bride to send the nurse at twilight faileth not, [hooks.
To whom the bridegroom given hath the ladder that he got.
And then to watch for him appointeth her an hour;
For whether Fortune smile on him, or if she list to lower,
He will not miss to come to his appointed place,   819
Where wont he was to take by stealth the view of Juliet's face.
How long these lovers thought the lasting of the day,
Let other judge that wonted are like passions to assay:
For my part, I do guess each hour seems twenty year:
So that I deem, if they might have, as of Alcume we hear,
The sun bound to their will, if they the heavens might guide,
Black shade of night and doubled dark should straight all over
    Th' appointed hour is come; he, clad in rich array, [hide.
Walks toward his desiréd home: good fortune guide his way.
Approaching near the place from whence his heart had life,
So light he wox, he leapt the wall, and there he spied his wife,
Who in the window watched the coming of her lord; 831
Where she so surely had made fast the ladder made of cord,
That dangerless her spouse the chamber window climbs,
Where he ere then had wished himself above ten thousand
The windows close are shut; else look they for no guest; [times.
To light the waxen quariers, the ancient nurse is pressed,
Which Juliet had before preparéd to be light,   837
That she at pleasure might behold her husband's beauty
A kerchief white as snow ware Juliet on her head, [bright.
Such as she wonted was to wear, attire meet for the bed.

As soon as she him spied, about his neck she clung,   841
And by her long and slender arms a great while there she
A thousand times she kissed, and him unkissed again, [hung.
Ne could she speak a word to him, though would she ne'er
And like betwixt his arms to faint his lady is;   [so fain.
She fets a sigh and clappeth close her closéd mouth to his;
And ready then to sownd she lookéd ruthfully,
That lo, it made him both at once to live and eke to die.
These piteous painful pangs were haply overpast,   849
And she unto herself again returnéd home at last.   [part,
Then, through her troubled breast, even from the farthest
An hollow sigh, a messenger, she sendeth from her heart.
O Romeus, quoth she, in whom all virtues shine,   [mine
Welcome thou art into this place, where from these eyes of
Such teary streams did flow, that I suppose well-nigh 855
The source of all my bitter tears is altogether dry.
Absence so pined my heart, which on thy presence fed,
And of thy safety and thy health so much I stood in dread.
But now what is decreed by fatal destiny,
I force it not; let Fortune do, and death, their worst to me.
Full recompensed am I for all my passéd harms,   861
In that the Gods have granted me to clasp thee in mine arms.
The crystal tears began to stand in Romeus' eyes,
When he unto his lady's words 'gan answer in this wise:
    'Though cruel Fortune be so much my deadly foe, 865
That I ne can by lively proof cause thee, fair dame, to know
How much I am by love enthralléd unto thee,
Ne yet what mighty power thou hast, by thy desert, on me,

Ne torments that for thee I did ere this endure,
Yet of thus much, ne will I feign, I may thee well assure ;
The least of many pains which of thy absence sprung,   871
More painfully than death itself my tender heart hath wrung.
Ere this, one death had reft a thousand deaths away,
But life prolongéd was by hope of this desiréd day ;
Which so just tribute pays of all my passéd moan,   875
That I as well contented am as if myself alone
Did from the Ocean reign unto the sea of Ind.
Wherefore now let us wipe away old cares out of our mind.
For as the wretched state is now redressed at last,
So is it skill behind our back the curséd care to cast.   880
Since Fortune of her grace hath place and time assigned,
Where we with pleasure may content our uncontented mind,
In Lethes hide we deep all grief and all annoy,   [joy.
Whilst we do bathe in bliss, and fill our hungry hearts with
And, for the time to come, let be our busy care   885
So wisely to direct our love, as no wight else be ware ;
Lest envious foes by force despoil our new delight,
And us throw back from happy state to more unhappy plight.'
Fair Juliet began to answer what he said,   [stayed.
But forth in haste the old nurse stepped, and so her answer
'Who takes not time,' quoth she, 'when time well offered is,
Another time shall seek for time, and yet of time shall miss.
And when occasion serves, whoso doth let it slip,
Is worthy sure, if I might judge, of lashes with a whip.
Wherefore if each of you hath harmed the other so,   895
And each of you hath been the cause of other's wailéd woe,

D

Lo here a field'—she showed a field-bed ready dight—
'Where you may, if you list, in arms revenge yourself by fight.'
Whereto these lovers both 'gan easily assent,   [went,
And to the place of mild revenge with pleasant cheer they
Where they were left alone—the nurse is gone to rest— 901
How can this be?   They restless lie, ne yet they feel unrest.
I grant that I envy the bliss they livéd in;
Oh that I might have found the like, I wish it for no sin,
But that I might as well with pen their joys depaint,   905
As heretofore I have displayed their secret hidden plaint.
Of shivering care and dread I have felt many a fit,
But Fortune such delight as theirs did never grant me yet.
By proof no certain truth can I unhappy write,
But what I guess by likelihood, that dare I to indite.   910
The blindfold goddess that with frowning face doth fray,
And from their seat the mighty kings throws down with head-
Beginneth now to turn to these her smiling face;   [long sway,
Needs must they taste of great delight, so much in Fortune's
If Cupid, god of love, be god of pleasant sport,   [grace.
I think, O Romeus, Mars himself envies thy happy sort.
Ne Venus justly might, as I suppose, repent,   917
If in thy stead, O Juliet, this pleasant time she spent.
    Thus pass they forth the night, in sport, in jolly game;
The hastiness of Phœbus' steeds in great despite they blame.
And now the virgin's fort hath warlike Romeus got,   921
In which as yet no breach was made by force of cannon shot,
And now in ease he doth possess the hopéd place: [embrace.
How glad was he, speak you that may your lover's parts

The marriage thus made up, and both the parties pleased,
The nigh approach of day's return these seely fools dis-eased.
And for they might no while in pleasure pass their time,
Ne leisure had they much to blame the hasty morning's crime,
With friendly kiss in arms of her his leave he takes, 929
And every other night, to come, a solemn oath he makes,
By one self mean, and eke to come at one self hour:
And so he doth, till Fortune list to sauce his sweet with sour.
But who is he that can his present state assure?
And say unto himself, thy joys shall yet a day endure? 934
So wavering Fortune's wheel, her changes be so strange;
And every wight y-thrallèd is by Fate unto her change,
Who reigns so over all, that each man hath his part
(Although not aye, perchance, alike) of pleasure and of smart.
For after many joys some feel but little pain,
And from that little grief they turn to happy joy again.
But other some there are, that, living long in woe, 941
At length they be in quiet ease, but long abide not so;
Whose grief is much increased by mirth that went before,
Because the sudden change of things doth make it seem the
Of this unlucky sort our Romeus is one, [more.
For all his hap turns to mishap, and all his mirth to moan.
And joyful Juliet another leaf must turn; 947
As wont she was, her joys bereft, she must begin to mourn.
 The summer of their bliss doth last a month or twain,
But winter's blast with speedy foot doth bring the fall again.
Whom glorious Fortune erst had heavèd to the skies, 951
By envious Fortune overthrown, on earth now grovelling lies.

She paid their former grief with pleasure's doubled gain,
But now for pleasure's usury, tenfold redoubleth pain.

The prince could never cause those households so agree,
But that some sparkles of their wrath as yet remaining be;
Which lie this while raked up in ashes pale and dead,   957
Till time do serve that they again in wasting flame may spread.
At holiest times, men say, most heinous crimes are done;
The morrow after Easter day the mischief new begun.   960
A band of Capulets did meet—my heart it rues!—
Within the walls, by Purser's gate, a band of Montagues.
The Capulets, as chief, a young man have chose out,
Best exercised in feats of arms, and noblest of the rout,
Our Juliet's uncle's son, that clepéd was Tybalt;   965
He was of body tall and strong, and of his courage halt.
They need no trumpet sound to bid them give the charge,
So loud he cried with strainéd voice and mouth outstretchéd
      large :
'Now, now,' quod he, 'my friends, ourself so let us wreak,
That of this day's revenge and us our children's heirs may
      speak.   970
Now once for all let us their swelling pride assuage ;
Let none of them escape alive.'   Then he, with furious rage,
And they with him, gave charge upon their present foes,
And then forthwith a skirmish great upon this fray arose.
For, lo, the Montagues thought shame away to fly,   975
And rather than to live with shame, with praise did choose
The words that Tybalt used to stir his folk to ire,   [to die.
Have in the breasts of Montagues kindled a furious fire.

With lions' hearts they fight, warely themself defend; 979
To wound his foe, his present wit and force each one doth
This furious fray is long on each side stoutly fought, [bend.
That whether part had got the worst, full doubtful were the
The noise hereof anon throughout the town doth fly, [thought.
And parts are taken on every side; both kindreds thither hie.
Here one doth gasp for breath, his friend bestrideth him;
And he hath lost a hand, and he another maiméd limb,
His leg is cut whilst he strikes at another full, [crackéd skull.
And whom he would have thrust quite through, hath cleft his
Their valiant hearts forbode their foot to give the ground;
With unappalléd cheer they took full deep and doubtful
    wound. 990
Thus foot by foot long while, and shield to shield set fast,
One foe doth make another faint, but makes him not aghast.
And whilst this noise is rife in every townsman's ear, [hear.
Eke, walking with his friends, the noise doth woeful Romeus
With speedy foot he runs unto the fray apace; [place.
With him, those few that were with him he leadeth to the
They pity much to see the slaughter made so great, [street.
That wetshod they might stand in blood on either side the
'Part, friends,' said he; 'Part, friends—help, friends, to part
    the fray,'
And to the rest, 'Enough,' he cries, 'Now time it is to stay.
God's farther wrath you stir, beside the hurt you feel, 1001
And with this new uproar confound all this our common weal.'
But they so busy are in fight, so eager and fiërce, [pierce.
That through their ears his sage advice no leisure had to

Then leapt he in the throng, to part and bar the blows
As well of those that were his friends, as of his deadly foes.
As soon as Tybalt had our Romeus espied,   [to side;
He threw a thrust at him that would have passed from side
But Romeus ever went, doubting his foes, well armed, [harmed.
So that the sword, kept out by mail, hath nothing Romeus
'Thou dost me wrong,' quoth he, 'for I but part the fray;
Not dread, but other weighty cause my hasty hand doth stay.
Thou art the chief of thine, the noblest eke thou art, 1013
Wherefore leave off thy malice now, and help these folk to
Many are hurt, some slain, and some are like to die.' [part.
    'No, coward, traitor boy,' quoth he, 'straightway I mind to
Whether thy sugared talk, and tongue so smoothly filed, [try,
Against the force of this my sword shall serve thee for a shield.
And then at Romeus' head a blow he strake so hard, 1019
That might have clove him to the brain but for his cunning
It was but lent to him that could repay again,   [ward.
And give him death for interest, a well forborne gain.
Right as a forest boar, that lodgéd in the thick,
Pinchéd with dog, or else with spear y-prickéd to the quick,
His bristles stiff upright upon his back doth set,   1025
And in his foamy mouth his sharp and crooked tusks doth
Or as a lion wild that rampeth in his rage,   [whet;
His whelps bereft, whose fury can no weaker beast assuage;
Such seeméd Romeus in every other's sight,   [fight.
When he him shope, of wrong received t' avenge himself by
Even as two thunderbolts thrown down out of the sky, [fly;
That through the air, the massy earth, and seas, have power to

So met these two, and while they change a blow or twain,
Our Romeus thrust him through the throat, and so is Tybalt
Lo, here the end of those that stir a deadly strife :   [slain.
Who thirsteth after other's death, himself hath lost his life.
The Capulets are quailed by Tybalt's overthrow,   1037
The courage of the Montagues by Romeus' sight doth grow.
The townsmen waxen strong, the Prince doth send his force ;
The fray hath end.   The Capulets do bring the breathless
Before the Prince, and crave that cruel deadly pain   [corse
May be the guerdon of his fault, that hath their kinsman slain.
The Montagues do plead their Romeus void of fault ; 1043
The lookers-on do say, the fight begun was by Tybalt.
The Prince doth pause, and then gives sentence in a while,
That Romeus for slaying him should go into exile.
His foes would have him hanged, or sterve in prison strong ;
His friends do think, but dare not say, that Romeus hath
              wrong.   1048
Both households straight are charged on pain of losing life,
Their bloody weapons laid aside, to cease the stirréd strife.
This common plague is spread through all the town anon,
From side to side the town is filled with murmur and with
For Tybalt's hasty death bewailéd was of some,   [moan,
Both for his skill in feats of arms, and for, in time to come
He should, had this not chanced, been rich and of great power,
To help his friends, and serve the state ; which hope within
              an hour   1056
Was wasted quite, and he, thus yielding up his breath, [death.
More than he holp the town in life, hath harmed it by his

And other some bewail, but ladies most of all,
The luckless lot by Fortune's guilt that is so late befall,
Without his fault, unto the seely Romeus;　　　1061
For whilst that he from native land shall live exiléd thus,
From heavenly beauty's light and his well-shapéd parts,
The sight of which was wont, fair dames, to glad your youth-
Shall you be banished quite, and till he do return, [ful hearts,
What hope have you to joy, what hope to cease to mourn?
This Romeus was born so much in heaven's grace,　　1067
Of Fortune and of Nature so beloved, that in his face,
Beside the heavenly beauty glist'ring aye so bright,
And seemly grace that wonted so to glad the seër's sight,
A certain charm was graved by Nature's secret art,　1071
That virtue had to draw to it the love of many a heart.
So every one doth wish to bear a part of pain,
That he reléaséd of exile might straight return again.
But how doth mourn among the mourners Juliet! [she fet!
How doth she bathe her breast in tears! What deep sighs doth
How doth she tear her hair! Her weed how doth she rent!
How fares the lover hearing of her lover's banishment! 1078
How wails she Tybalt's death, whom she had loved so well!
Her hearty grief and piteous plaint, cunning I want to tell.
For delving deeply now in depth of deep despair,　　1081
With wretched sorrow's cruel sound she fills the empty air;
And to the lowest hell down falls her heavy cry,
And up unto the heaven's height her piteous plaint doth fly.
The waters and the woods of sighs and sobs resound,
And from the hard resounding rocks her sorrows do rebound.

Eke from her teary eyne down rainéd many a shower,
That in the garden where she walked might water herb and
But when at length she saw herself outragéd so,   [flower.
Unto her chamber straight she hied ; there, overcharged with
Upon her stately bed her painful parts she threw,   [woe,
And in so wondrous wise began her sorrows to renew,   1092
That sure no heart so hard, but it of flint had bin,
But would have rued the piteous plaint that she did languish
Then rapt out of herself, whilst she on every side   [in.
Did cast her restless eye, at length the window she espied,
Through which she had with joy seen Romeus many a time,
Which oft the vent'rous knight was wont for Juliet's sake to
    She cried, 'O cursed window, accursed be every pane, [climb.
Through which, alas, too soon I raught the cause of life and
If by thy mean I have some slight delight received,   [bane ;
Or else such fading pleasure as by Fortune straight was reaved,
Hast thou not made me pay a tribute rigorous   1103
Of heapéd grief and lasting care, and sorrows dolorous,
That these my tender parts, which needful strength do lack
To bear so great unwieldy load upon so weak a back,
Oppressed with weight of cares and with these sorrows rife,
At length must open wide to death the gates of loathéd life ;
That so my weary sprite may somewhere else unload   1109
His deadly load, and free from thrall may seek elsewhere
For pleasant, quiet ease and for assuréd rest,   [abode
Which I as yet could never find but for my more unrest ?
O Romeus, when first we both acquainted were,
When to thy painted promises I lent my list'ning ear,

Which to the brinks you filled with many a solemn oath,
And I them judged empty of guile, and fraughted full of
I thought you rather would continue our good will, [troth,
And seek t' appease our fathers' strife, which daily groweth
I little weened you would have sought occasion how   [still.
By such an heinous act to break the peace and eke your vow ;
Whereby your bright renown all whole y-clipséd is,   1121
And I unhappy, husbandless, of comfort robbed and bliss.
But if you did so much the blood of Capels thirst,
Why have you often sparéd mine ?—mine might have
        quenched it first.
Since that so many times and in so secret place,   1125
Where you were wont with veil of love to hide your hatred's
My doubtful life hath happed by fatal doom to stand [face,
In mercy of your cruel heart, and of your bloody hand.
What ?—seemed the conquest which you got of me so small ?
What ?—seemed it not enough that I, poor wretch, was
        made your thrall ?   1130
But that you must increase it with that kinsman's blood,
Which for his worth and love to me, most in my favour stood ?
Well, go henceforth elsewhere, and seek another while
Some other as unhappy as I, by flattery to beguile.   1134
And, where I come, see that you shun to show your face,
For your excuse within my heart shall find no resting place.
And I that now, too late, my former fault repent,
Will so the rest of weary life with many tears lament,
That soon my joiceless corpse shall yield up banished breath,
And where on earth it restless lived, in earth seek rest by death.'

These said, her tender heart, by pain oppresséd sore, 1141
Restrained her tears, and forced her tongue to keep her talk
And then as still she was, as if in sownd she lay, [in store;
And then again, wroth with herself, with feeble voice 'gan
  'Ah, cruel murthering tongue, murth'rer of others' fame, [say:
How durst thou once attempt to touch the honour of his name?
Whose deadly foes do yield him due and earnéd praise;
For though his freedom be bereft, his honour not decays.
Why blam'st thou Romeus for slaying of Tybalt, 1149
Since he is guiltless quite of all, and Tybalt bears the fault?
Whither shall he, alas, poor banished man, now fly?
What place of succour shall he seek beneath the starry sky?
Since she pursueth him, and him defames by wrong,
That in distress should be his fort, and only rampire strong.
Receive the recompense, O Romeus, of thy wife, 1155
Who, for she was unkind herself, doth offer up her life,
In flames of ire, in sighs, in sorrow and in ruth,
So to revenge the crime she did commit against thy truth.'
These said, she could no more; her senses all 'gan fail,
And deadly pangs began straightway her tender heart assail;
Her limbs she stretchéd forth, she drew no more her breath:
Who had been there might well have seen the signs of present
The nurse that knew no cause why she absented her, [death.
Did doubt lest that some sudden grief too much tormented her.
Each where but where she was the careful beldam sought;
Last, of the chamber where she lay she haply her bethought;
Where she with piteous eye her nurse-child did behold,
Her limbs stretched out, her outward parts as any marble cold.

The nurse supposed that she had paid to death her debt,
And then, as she had lost her wits, she cried to Juliet: 1170
'Ah, my dear heart,' quoth she, 'how grieveth me thy death?
Alas, what cause hast thou thus soon to yield up living breath?'
But while she handled her, and chaféd every part,   [heart,
She knew there was some spark of life by beating of her
So that a thousand times she called upon her name; 1175
There is no way to help a trance but she hath tried the same:
She openeth wide her mouth, she stoppeth close her nose,
She bendeth down her breast, she wrings her fingers and her
And on her bosom cold she layeth clothés hot;   [toes,
A warméd and a wholesome juice she poureth down her throat.

At length doth Juliet heave faintly up her eyes,   [spies.
And then she stretcheth forth her arm, and then her nurse she
But when she was awaked from her unkindly trance, 1183
'Why dost thou trouble me,' quoth she, 'what drave thee, with
    mischance,
To come to see my sprite forsake my breathless corse?
Go hence, and let me die, if thou have on my smart
    remorse.
For who would see her friend to live in deadly pain?
Alas, I see my grief begun for ever will remain.
Or who would seek to live, all pleasure being past? 1189
My mirth is done, my mourning moan for aye is like to last.
Wherefore since that there is none other remedy,   [die.'
Come, gentle death, and rive my heart at once, and let me
The nurse with trickling tears, to witness inward smart,
With hollow sigh fetched from the depth of her appalléd heart,

Thus spake to Juliet, y-clad with ugly care: 1195
  'Good lady mine, I do not know what makes you thus to
Ne yet the cause of your unmeasured heaviness.   [fare;
But of this one I you assure, for care and sorrow's stress,
This hour large and more I thought, so God me save, 1199
That my dead corpse should wait on yours to your untimely
  'Alas, my tender nurse and trusty friend,' quoth she, [grave.'
'Art thou so blind that with thine eye thou canst not easely
The lawful cause I have to sorrow and to mourn,   [see
Since those the which I held most dear, I have at once forlorn.'
Her nurse then answered thus: 'Methinks it sits you ill
To fall in these extremities that may you guiltless spill.
For when the storms of care and troubles do arise,
Then is the time for men to know the foolish from the wise.
You are accounted wise, a fool am I your nurse; 1209
But I see not how in like case I could behave me worse.
Tybalt your friend is dead; what, ween you by your tears
To call him back again? think you that he your crying
You shall perceive the fault, if it be justly tried,   [hears?
Of his so sudden death, was in his rashness and his pride.
Would you that Romeus himself had wrongéd so, 1215
To suffer himself causeless to be outraged of his foe,
To whom in no respect he ought a place to give?
Let it suffice to thee, fair dame, that Romeus doth live,
And that there is good hope that he, within a while,
With greater glory shall be called home from his hard exile.
How well y-born he is, thyself, I know, canst tell, 1221
By kindred strong, and well allied, of all belovéd well.

With patience arm thyself, for though that Fortune's crime,
Without your fault, to both your griefs, depart you for a time,
I dare say, for amends of all your present pain,   1225
She will restore your own to you, within a month or twain,
With such contented ease as never erst you had;
Wherefore rejoice a while in hope, and be ne more so sad.
And that I may discharge your heart of heavy care,
A certain way I have found out, my pains ne will I spare,
To learn his present state, and what in time to come 1231
He minds to do; which known by me, you shall know all and
But that I dread the whilst your sorrows will you quell, [some.
Straight would I hie where he doth lurk, to Friar Laurence'
But if you 'gin eftsoons, as erst you did, to mourn,   [cell.
Whereto go I? you will be dead, before I thence return.
So I shall spend in waste my time and busy pain.   1237
So unto you, your life once lost, good answer comes in vain;
So shall I rid myself with this sharp-pointed knife;
So shall you cause your parents dear wax weary of their life;
So shall your Romeus, despising lively breath,   1241
With hasty foot, before his time, run to untimely death.
Where, if you can awhile, by reason, rage suppress,
I hope at my return to bring the salve of your distress.
Now choose to have me here a partner of your pain, 1245
Or promise me to feed on hope till I return again.'

   Her mistress sends her forth, and makes a grave behest
With reason's reign to rule the thoughts that rage within her
When hugy heaps of harms are heaped before her eyes, [breast.
Then vanish they by hope of 'scape; and thus the lady lies

'Twixt well assuréd trust, and doubtful lewd despair: 1251
Now black and ugly be her thoughts; now seem they white
    and fair.
As oft in summer tide black clouds do dim the sun,
And straight again in clearest sky his restless steeds do run ;
So Juliet's wand'ring mind y-clouded is with woe,   1255
And by and by her hasty thought the woes doth overgo.
    But now is time to tell, whilst she was tosséd thus,
What winds did drive or haven did hold her lover, Romeus.
When he had slain his foe that 'gan this deadly strife, 1259
And saw the furious fray had end by ending Tybalt's life,
He fled the sharp revenge of those that yet did live,
And doubting much what penal doom the troubled prince
    might give,
He sought somewhere unseen to lurk a little space,
And trusty Laurence' secret cell he thought the surest place.
In doubtful hap aye best a trusty friend is tried ;   1265
The friendly friar in this distress doth grant his friend to
A secret place he hath, well sealéd round about,   [hide.
The mouth of which so close is shut, that none may find it
But room there is to walk, and place to sit and rest,   [out ;
Beside a bed to sleep upon, full soft and trimly drest. 1270
The floor is plankéd so, with mats it is so warm,   [to harm.
That neither wind nor smoky damps have power him aught
Where he was wont in youth his fair friends to bestow,
There now he hideth Romeus, whilst forth he goeth to know
Both what is said and done, and what appointed pain, 1275
Is publishéd by trumpet's sound ; then home he hies again.

By this, unto his cell the nurse with speedy pace
Was come the nearest way; she sought no idle resting place.
The friar sent home the news of Romeus' certain health,
And promise made, what so befell, he should that night by
Come to his wonted place, that they in needful wise [stealth
Of their affairs in time to come might thoroughly devise.
Those joyful news the nurse brought home with merry joy;
And now our Juliet joys to think she shall her love enjoy.
The friar shuts fast his door, and then to him beneath,
That waits to hear the doubtful news of life or else of death,
'Thy hap,' quoth he, 'is good, danger of death is none,
But thou shalt live, and do full well, in spite of spiteful fone.
This only pain for thee was erst proclaimed aloud,   1289
A banished man, thou may'st thee not within Verona shroud.'
    These heavy tidings heard, his golden locks he tare,
And like a frantic man hath torn the garments that he ware.
And as the smitten deer in brakes is walt'ring found, [ground.
So wal'treth he, and with his breast doth beat the trodden
He rises eft, and strikes his head against the walls,   1295
He falleth down again, and loud for hasty death he calls.
'Come speedy death,' quoth he, 'the readiest leech in love;
Since nought can else beneath the sun the ground of grief
        remove,
Of loathsome life break down the hated, staggering stays,
Destroy, destroy at once the life that faintly yet decays. 1300
But you, fair dame, in whom dame Nature did devise
With cunning hand to work that might seem wondrous in
        our eyes,

For you, I pray the Gods, your pleasures to increase,
And all mishap, with this my death, for evermore to cease.
And mighty Jove with speed of justice bring them low,
Whose lofty pride, without our guilt, our bliss doth overblow.
And Cupid grant to those their speedy wrongs' redress,
That shall bewail my cruel death and pity her distress.'
Therewith a cloud of sighs he breathed into the skies, 1309
And two great streams of bitter tears ran from his swollen
    eyes.
These things the ancient friar with sorrow saw and heard,
Of such beginning, eke the end, the wise man greatly feared.
But lo, he was so weak, by reason of his age,
That he ne could by force repress the rigour of his rage.
His wise and friendly words he speaketh to the air, 1315
For Romeus so vexéd is with care and with despair,
That no advice can pierce his close forestoppéd ears;
So now the friar doth take his part in shedding ruthful tears.
With colour pale and wan, with arms full hard y-fold,
With woeful cheer his wailing friend he standeth to behold.
And then our Romeus with tender hands y-wrung, 1321
With voice with plaint made hoarse, with sobs, and with a
    falt'ring tongue,
Renewed with novel moan the dolours of his heart;
His outward dreary cheer bewrayed his store of inward smart.
First Nature did he blame, the author of his life, 1325
In which his joys had been so scant, and sorrows aye so rife;
The time and place of birth he fiercely did reprove,
He criéd out, with open mouth, against the stars above;

E

The fatal sisters three, he said, had done him wrong,
The thread that should not have been spun, they had drawn
    forth too long.   1330
He wishéd that he had before this time been born,
Or that as soon as he wan light, his life he had forlorn.
His nurse he curséd, and the hand that gave him pap,
The midwife eke with tender grip that held him in her lap;
And then did he complain on Venus' cruel son,   1335
Who led him first unto the rocks which he should warely
    shun :
By means whereof he lost both life and liberty,
And died a hundred times a day, and yet could never die.
Love's troubles lasten long, the joys he gives are short ;
He forceth not a lover's pain, their earnest is his sport. 1340
A thousand things and more I here let pass to write,
Which unto Love this woeful man did speak in great despite.
On Fortune eke he railed, he called her deaf and blind,
Unconstant, fond, deceitful, rash, unruthful, and unkind.
And to himself he laid a great part of the fault,   1345
For that he slew and was not slain, in fighting with Tybalt.
He blaméd all the world, and all he did defy,
But Juliet for whom he lived, for whom eke would he die.
    When after raging fits appeaséd was his rage,
And when his passions, pouréd forth, 'gan partly to assuage,
So wisely did the friar unto his tale reply,   1351
That he straight caréd for his life, that erst had care to die.
  'Art thou,' quoth he, 'a man ?   Thy shape saith, so thou art ;
Thy crying, and thy weeping eyes denote a woman's heart.

For manly reason is quite from off thy mind outchased, 1355
And in her stead affections lewd and fancies highly placed:
So that I stood in doubt, this hour, at the least,
If thou a man or woman wert, or else a brutish beast.
A wise man in the midst of troubles and distress [redress.
Still stands not wailing present harm, but seeks his harm's
As when the winter flaws with dreadful noise arise, 1361
And heave the foamy swelling waves up to the starry skies,
So that the bruiséd bark in cruel seas betost,
Despaireth of the happy haven, in danger to be lost,
The pilot bold at helm, cries, "Mates, strike now your sail,"
And turns her stem into the waves that strongly her assail;
Then driven hard upon the bare and wrackful shore, 1367
In greater danger to be wracked than he had been before,
He seeth his ship full right against the rock to run,
But yet he doth what lieth in him the perilous rock to shun:
Sometimes the beaten boat, by cunning government, 1371
The anchors lost, the cables broke, and all the tackle spent,
The rudder smitten off, and overboard the mast,
Doth win the long desiréd port, the stormy danger past:
But if the master dread, and overpressed with woe 1375
Begin to wring his hands, and lets the guiding rudder go,
The ship rents on the rock, or sinketh in the deep,
And eke the coward drenchéd is: So, if thou still beweep
And seek not how to help the changes that do chance, 1379
Thy cause of sorrow shall increase, thou cause of thy mis-
Other account thee wise, prove not thyself a fool; [chance.
Now put in practice lessons learned of old in wisdom's school.

The wise man saith, "Beware thou double not thy pain,
For one perhaps thou may'st abide, but hardly suffer twain."
As well we ought to seek things hurtful to decrease,   1385
As to endeavour helping things by study to increase.
The praise of true freedom in wisdom's bondage lies,
He winneth blame whose deeds be fond, although his words
Sickness the body's gaol, grief gaol is of the mind, [be wise.
If thou canst 'scape from heavy grief, true freedom shalt thou
Fortune can fill nothing so full of hearty grief,   [find.
But in the same a constant mind finds solace and relief.
Virtue is always thrall to troubles and annoy,   1393
But wisdom in adversity finds cause of quiet joy.
And they most wretched are that know no wretchedness,
And after great extremity mishaps aye waxen less.
Like as there is no weal but wastes away sometime,
So every kind of wailéd woe will wear away in time.
If thou wilt master quite the troubles that thee spill,
Endeavour first by reason's help to master witless will. 1400
A sundry med'cine hath each sundry faint disease,
But patience, a common salve, to every wound gives ease.
The world is alway full of chances and of change, [strange.
Wherefore the change of chance must not seem to a wise man
For tickel Fortune doth, in changing, but her kind,   1405
But all her changes cannot change a steady constant mind.
Though wavering Fortune turn from thee her smiling face,
And Sorrow seek to set himself in banished Pleasure's place,
Yet may thy marréd state be mended in a while,   [smile,
And she eftsoons that frowneth now, with pleasant cheer shall

For as her happy state no long while standeth sure, 1411
Even so the heavy plight she brings, not always doth endure.
What need so many words to thee that art so wise?
Thou better canst advise thyself, than I can thee advise.
Wisdom, I see, is vain, if thus in time of need 1415
A wise man's wit unpractiséd doth stand him in no stede.
I know thou hast some cause of sorrow and of care,
But well I wot thou hast no cause thus franticly to fare.
Affection's foggy mist thy feebled sight doth blind; 1419
But if that reason's beams again might shine into thy mind,
If thou would'st view thy state with an indifferent eye, [cry.
I think thou would'st condemn thy plaint, thy sighing, and thy
With valiant hand thou mad'st thy foe yield up his breath,
Thou hast escaped his sword and eke the laws that threaten
By thy escape thy friends are fraughted full of joy, [death.
And by his death thy deadly foes are laden with annoy.
Wilt thou with trusty friends of pleasure take some part?
Or else to please thy hateful foes be partner of their smart?
Why cry'st thou out on love? Why dost thou blame thy fate?
Why dost thou so cry after death? Thy life why dost thou
    hate? 1430
Dost thou repent the choice that thou so late didst choose?
Love is thy Lord; thou ought'st obey and not thy prince
    accuse.
For thou hast found, thou know'st, great favour in his sight.
He granted thee, at thy request, thy only heart's delight.
So that the gods envied the bliss thou lived'st in; 1435
To give to such unthankful men is folly and a sin.

Methinks I hear thee say, the cruel banishment
Is only cause of thy unrest; only thou dost lament
That from thy native land and friends thou must depart,
Enforced to fly from her that hath the keeping of thy heart:
And so oppressed with weight of smart that thou dost feel,
Thou dost complain of Cupid's brand, and Fortune's turning
Unto a valiant heart there is no banishment,   [wheel.
All countries are his native soil beneath the firmament.
As to the fish the sea, as to the fowl the air,   1445
So is like pleasant to the wise each place of his repair.
Though froward Fortune chase thee hence into exile,
With doubled honour shall she call thee home within a while.
Admit thou should'st abide abroad a year or twain,   [pain?
Should so short absence cause so long and eke so grievous
Though thou ne may'st thy friends here in Verona see, 1451
They are not banished Mantua, where safely thou may'st be.
Thither they may resort, though thou resort not hither,
And there in surety may you talk of your affairs together.
Yea, but this while, alas, thy Juliet must thou miss,   1455
The only pillar of thy health, and anchor of thy bliss.
Thy heart thou leav'st with her, when thou dost hence depart,
And in thy breast incloséd bear'st her tender friendly heart.
But if thou rue so much to leave the rest behind,   1459
With thought of passéd joys content thy uncontented mind.
So shall the moan decrease wherewith thy mind doth melt,
Comparéd to the heavenly joys which thou hast often felt.
He is too nice a weakling that shrinketh at a shower,
And he unworthy of the sweet, that tasteth not the sour.

Call now again to mind thy first consuming flame, 1465
How didst thou vainly burn in love of an unloving dame?
Hadst thou not wellnigh wept quite out thy swelling eyne?
Did not thy parts, fordone with pain, languish away and
Those griefs and others like were haply overpast, [pine?
And thou in height of Fortune's wheel well placéd at the last!
From whence thou art now fall'n, that, raiséd up again,
With greater joy a greater while in pleasure may'st thou reign.
Compare the present while with times y-past before, 1473
And think that Fortune hath for thee great pleasure yet in
The whilst, this little wrong receive thou patiently, [store.
And what of force must needs be done, that do thou willingly.
Folly it is to fear that thou canst not avoid,
And madness to desire it much that cannot be enjoyed.
To give to Fortune place, not aye deserveth blame,
But skill it is, according to the times thyself to frame.' 1480
    Whilst to this skilful lore he lent his list'ning ears, [tears.
His sighs are stopped and stoppéd are the conduits of his
As blackest clouds are chased by winter's nimble wind,
So have his reasons chaséd care out of his careful mind.
As of a morning foul ensues an evening fair, 1485
So banished hope returneth home to banish his despair.
Now is affection's veil removéd from his eyes, [wise.
He seeth the path that he must walk, and reason makes him
For very shame the blood doth flash in both his cheeks,
He thanks the father for his lore, and farther aid he seeks.
He saith, that skill-less youth for counsel is unfit, 1491
And anger oft with hastiness are joined to want of wit;

But sound advice abounds in heads with hoarish hairs,
For wisdom is by practice won, and perfect made by years.
But aye from this time forth his ready bending will   1495
Shall be in awe and governéd by Friar Laurence' skill.
The governor is now right careful of his charge,
To whom he doth wisely discourse of his affairs at large.
He tells him how he shall depart the town unknown,
Both mindful of his friend's safety, and careful of his own;
How he shall guide himself, how he shall seek to win 1501
The friendship of the better sort, how warely to creep in
The favour of the Mantuan prince, and how he may
Appease the wrath of Escalus, and wipe the fault away;
The choler of his foes by gentle means t' assuage,   1505
Or else by force and practices to bridle quite their rage:
And last he chargeth him at his appointed hour
To go with manly, merry cheer unto his lady's bower,
And there with wholesome words to salve her sorrow's smart,
And to revive, if need require, her faint and dying heart.
    The old man's words have filled with joy our Romeus'
        breast,   1511
And eke the old wife's talk hath set our Juliet's heart at rest.
Whereto may I compare, O lovers, this your day?
Like days the painful mariners are wonted to assay;
For, beat with tempest great, when they at length espy 1515
Some little beam of Phœbus' light, that pierceth through
        the sky,
To clear the shadowed earth by clearness of his face, [race;
They hope that dreadless they shall run the remnant of their

Yea, they assure themself, and quite behind their back
They cast all doubt, and thank the gods for scaping of the
   wrack;   1520
But straight the boisterous winds with greater fury blow,
And overboard the broken mast the stormy blasts do throw;
The heavens large are clad with clouds as dark as hell,
And twice as high the striving waves begin to roar and swell;
With greater dangers dread the men are vexéd more, 1525
In greater peril of their life than they had been before.
 The golden sun was gone to lodge him in the west,
The full moon eke in yonder south had sent most men to
When restless Romeus and restless Juliet   [rest,
In wonted sort, by wonted mean, in Juliet's chamber met.
And from the window's top down had he leapéd scarce,
When she with arms outstretchéd wide so hard did him
   embrace,   1532
That wellnigh had the sprite, not forced by deadly force,
Flown unto death, before the time abandoning the corse,
Thus muët stood they both the eighth part of an hour,
And both would speak, but neither had of speaking any power;
But on his breast her head doth joyless Juliet lay,   1537
And on her slender neck his chin doth ruthful Romeus stay.
Their scalding sighs ascend, and by their cheeks down fall
Their trickling tears, as crystal clear, but bitterer far than
Then he, to end the grief which both they lived in, [gall.
Did kiss his love, and wisely thus his tale he did begin:
 'My Juliet, my love, my only hope and care,
To you I purpose not as now with length of words declare

The diverseness and eke the accidents so strange   1545
Of frail unconstant Fortune, that delighteth still in change;
Who in a moment heaves her friends up to the height [straight.
Of her swift-turning slippery wheel, then fleets her friendship
O wondrous change, even with the twinkling of an eye
Whom erst herself had rashly set in pleasant place so high,
The same in great despite down headlong doth she throw,
And while she treads and spurneth at the lofty state laid low,
More sorrow doth she shape within an hour's space,   1553
Than pleasure in an hundred years; so geason is her grace.
The proof whereof in me, alas, too plain appears,   [feres,
Whom tenderly my careful friends have fostered with my
In prosperous high degree, maintainéd so by fate,
That, as yourself did see, my foes envied my noble state.
One thing there was I did above the rest desire,   1559
To which as to the sovereign good by hope I would aspire.
That by our marriage mean we might within a while,
To work our perfect happiness, our parents reconcile:
That safely so we might, not stopped by sturdy strife, [life.
Unto the bounds that God hath set, guide forth our pleasant
But now, alack, too soon my bliss is overblown,   1565
And upside down my purpose and my enterprise are thrown.
And driven from my friends, of strangers must I crave;
Oh, grant it God, from dangers dread that I may surety have.
For lo, henceforth I must wander in lands unknown   1569
(So hard I find the Prince's doom), exiléd from mine own.
Which thing I have thought good to set before your eyes,
And to exhort you now to prove yourself a woman wise,

That patiently you bear my absent long abode,
For what above by fatal dooms decreéd is, that God'——
And more than this to say, it seeméd, he was bent,   1575
But Juliet in deadly grief, with brackish tears besprent,
Brake off his tale begun, and whilst his speech he stayed,
These selfsame words, or like to these, with dreary cheer she
    'Why, Romeus, can it be thou hast so hard a heart; [said:
So far removed from ruth; so far from thinking on my smart;
To leave me thus alone, thou cause of my distress,
Besiegéd with so great a camp of mortal wretchedness, 1582
That every hour now, and moment in a day,
A thousand times Death brags, as he would reave my life
Yet such is my mishap, O cruel destiny,   [away?
That still I live, and wish for death, but yet can never die;
So that just cause I have to think, as seemeth me,
That froward Fortune did of late with cruel Death agree
To lengthen loathéd life, to pleasure in my pain,
And triumph in my harm, as in the greatest hopéd gain.
And thou, the instrument of Fortune's cruel will,   1591
Without whose aid she can no way her tyrannous lust fulfil,
Art not a whit ashamed, as far as I can see,
To cast me off, when thou hast culled the better part of me.
Whereby, alas, too soon, I, seely wretch, do prove,   1595
That all the ancient sacred laws of friendship and of love
Are quelled and quenchéd quite, since he, on whom alway
My chief hope and my steady trust was wonted still to stay,
For whom I am become unto myself a foe,   [ship so.
Disdaineth me, his steadfast friend, and scorns my friend-

Nay, Romeus, nay, thou may'st of two things choose the
    one,
Either to see thy castaway, as soon as thou art gone,   1602
Headlong to throw herself down from the window's height,
And so to break her slender neck with all the body's weight,
Or suffer her to be companion of thy pain,
Whereso thou go, Fortune thee guide, till thou return again.
So wholly into thine transforméd is my heart,
That even as oft as I do think that thou and I shall part,
So oft, methinks, my life withdraws itself away,
Which I retain to no end else but to the end I may,   1610
In spite of all thy foes, thy present parts enjoy,
And in distress to bear with thee the half of thine annoy.
Wherefore, in humble sort, Romeus, I make request,
If ever tender pity yet were lodged in gentle breast,
Oh, let it now have place to rest within thy heart;   1615
Receive me as thy servant, and the fellow of thy smart.
Thy absence is my death, thy sight shall give me life;
But if perhaps thou stand in dread to lead me as a wife,
Art thou all counsel-less?   Canst thou no shift devise?
What letteth but in other weed I may myself disguise? 1620
What, shall I be the first?   Hath none done so ere this,
To 'scape the bondage of their friends? Thyself can answer,
    yes.
Or dost thou stand in doubt that I thy wife ne can
By service pleasure thee as much as may thy hiréd man?
Or is my loyalty of both accompted less?   1625
Perhaps thou fear'st lest I for gain forsake thee in distress.

What, hath my beauty now no power at all on you,
Whose brightness, force, and praise, sometime up to the skies
    you blew ?
My tears, my friendship and my pleasures done of old,
Shall they be quite forgot indeed ?'
                  When Romeus did behold   1630
The wildness of her look, her colour pale and dead,
The worst of all that might betide to her, he 'gan to dread ;
And once again he did in arms his Juliet take,
And kissed her with a loving kiss, and thus to her he spake :
  'Ah, Juliet,' quoth he, 'the mistress of my heart, 1635
For whom, even now, thy servant doth abide in deadly
Even for the happy days which thou desir'st to see, [smart,
And for the fervent friendship's sake that thou dost owe to
At once these fancies vain out of thy mind root out,   [me,
Except, perhaps, unto thy blame, thou fondly go about
To hasten forth my death, and to thine own to run, 1641
Which Nature's law and wisdom's lore teach every wight to
For, but thou change thy mind, I do foretell the end, [shun.
Thou shalt undo thyself for aye, and me thy trusty friend.
For why, thy absence known, thy father will be wroth,
And in his rage so narrowly he will pursue us both, 1646
That we shall try in vain to 'scape away by flight,
And vainly seek a lurking place to hide us from his sight.
Then we, found out and caught, quite void of strong defence,
Shall cruelly be punishéd for thy departure hence ;   1650
I as a ravisher, thou as a careless child,
I as a man who doth defile, thou as a maid defiled ;

Thinking to lead in ease a long contented life,   [wife,
Shall short our days by shameful death: but if, my loving
Thou banish from thy mind two foes that counsel hath,
That wont to hinder sound advice, rash hastiness and wrath;
If thou be bent t'obey the lore of reason's skill   1657
And wisely by her princely power suppress rebelling will,
If thou our safety seek, more than thine own delight,
Since surety stands in parting, and thy pleasures grow of sight,
Forbear the cause of joy, and suffer for a while,   1661
So shall I safely live abroad, and safe turn from exile,
So shall no slander's blot thy spotless life distain,
So shall thy kinsmen be unstirred, and I exempt from pain.
And think thou not, that aye the cause of care shall last;
These stormy broils shall overblow, much like a winter's
For Fortune changeth more than fickle fantasy;   [blast.
In nothing Fortune constant is save in unconstancy.
Her hasty running wheel is of a restless course,   [worse,
That turns the climbers headlong down, from better to the
And those that are beneath she heaveth up again: 1671
So we shall rise to pleasure's mount, out of the pit of pain.
Ere four months overpass, such order will I take,   [make,
And by my letters and my friends such means I mind to
That of my wand'ring race ended shall be the toil,   1675
And I called home with honour great unto my native soil.
But if I be condemned to wander still in thrall,
I will return to you, mine own, befall what may befall.
And then by strength of friends, and with a mighty hand,
From Verone will I carry thee into a foreign land,   1680

Not in man's weed disguised, or as one scarcely known,
But as my wife and only fere, in garment of thine own.
Wherefore repress at once the passions of thy heart, [smart.
And where there is no cause of grief, cause hope to heal thy
For of this one thing thou may'st well assuréd be,   1685
That nothing else but only death shall sunder me from thee.'
   The reasons that he made did seem of so great weight,
And had with her such force, that she to him 'gan answer
   'Dear sir, nought else wish I but to obey your will; [straight:
But sure whereso you go, your heart with me shall tarry still,
As sign and certain pledge, till here I shall you see,   1691
Of all the power that over you yourself did grant to me;
And in his stead take mine, the gage of my good will.—
One promise crave I at your hand, that grant me to fulfil;
Fail not to let me have, at Friar Laurence' hand,   1695
The tidings of your health, and how your doubtful case shall
And all the weary while that you shall spend abroad, [stand.
Cause me from time to time to know the place of your abode.'
His eyes did gush out tears, a sigh brake from his breast,
When he did grant and with an oath did vow to keep the hest.
   Thus these two lovers pass away the weary night,   1701
In pain and plaint, not, as they wont, in pleasure and delight.
But now, somewhat too soon, in farthest east arose
Fair Lucifer, the golden star that lady Venus chose;
Whose course appointed is with speedy race to run,   1705
A messenger of dawning day and of the rising sun.
Then fresh Aurora with her pale and silver glade
Did clear the skies, and from the earth had chaséd ugly shade.

When thou ne lookest wide, ne closely dost thou wink,
When Phœbus from our hemisphere in western wave doth sink,
What colour then the heavens do show unto thine eyes,
The same, or like, saw Romeus in farthest eastern skies.
As yet he saw no day, ne could he call it night,
With equal force decreasing dark fought with increasing light.
Then Romeus in arms his lady 'gan to fold,   1715
With friendly kiss, and ruthfully she 'gan her knight behold.
With solemn oath they both their sorrowful leave do take;
They swear no stormy troubles shall their steady friendship
Then careful Romeus again to cell returns,   [shake.
And in her chamber secretly our joyless Juliet mourns.
Now hugy clouds of care, of sorrow, and of dread,   1721
The clearness of their gladsome hearts hath wholly overspread.
When golden-crested Phœbus boasteth him in sky,
And under earth, to 'scape revenge, his deadly foe doth fly,
Then hath these lovers' day an end, their night begun,
For each of them to other is as to the world the sun, 1726
The dawning they shall see, ne summer any more,   [sore.
But blackfaced night with winter rough, ah, beaten over
   The weary watch discharged did hie them home to sleep,
The warders and the scouts were charged their place and course
And Verone gates awide the porters had set open,   [to keep,
When Romeus had of his affairs with Friar Laurence spoken.
Warely he walkéd forth, unknown of friend or foe,   1733
Clad like a merchant venturer, from top even to the toe.
He spurred apace, and came, withouten stop or stay,
To Mantua gates, where lighted down, he sent his man away

With words of comfort to his old afflicted sire;   1737
And straight, in mind to sojourn there, a lodging doth he hire,
And with the nobler sort he doth himself acquaint,
And of his open wrong received the duke doth hear his plaint.
He practiseth by friends for pardon of exile;   1741
The whilst he seeketh every way his sorrows to beguile.
But who forgets the coal that burneth in his breast?
Alas, his cares deny his heart the sweet desiréd rest;
No time finds he of mirth, he finds no place of joy,   1745
But everything occasion gives of sorrow and annoy.
For when in turning skies the heaven's lamps are light,
And from the other hemisphere fair Phœbus chaseth night,
When every man and beast hath rest from painful toil,
Then in the breast of Romeus his passions 'gin to boil.   1750
Then doth he wet with tears the couch whereon he lies,
And then his sighs the chamber fill, and out aloud he cries
Against the restless stars in rolling skies that range,
Against the fatal sisters three, and Fortune full of change.
Each night a thousand times he calleth for the day,   1755
He thinketh Titan's restless steeds of restiness do stay;
Or that at length they have some baiting place found out,
Or, guided ill, have lost their way and wandered far about.
While thus in idle thoughts the weary time he spendeth,
The night hath end, but not with night the plaint of night
Is he accompanied?   Is he in place alone?   [he endeth.
In company he wails his harm, apart he maketh moan:
For if his feres rejoice, what cause hath he to joy,   [enjoy?
That wanteth still his chief delight, while they their loves

But if with heavy cheer they show their inward grief, 1765
He waileth most his wretchedness that is of wretches chief.
When he doth hear abroad the praise of ladies blown, [own.
Within his thought he scorneth them, and doth prefer his
When pleasant songs he hears, while others do rejoice,
The melody of music doth stir up his mourning voice.
But if in secret place he walk somewhere alone,   1771
The place itself and secretness redoubleth all his moan.
Then speaks he to the beasts, to feathered fowls and trees,
Unto the earth, the clouds, and to whatso beside he sees.
To them he shew'th his smart, as though they reason had.
Each thing may cause his heaviness, but nought may make
And, weary of the day, again he calleth night,   [him glad,
The sun he curseth, and the hour when first his eyes saw light.
And as the night and day their course do interchange, 1779
So doth our Romeus' nightly cares for cares of day exchange.

   In absence of her knight the lady no way could   [would;
Keep truce between her griefs and her, though ne'er so fain she
And though with greater pain she cloakéd sorrow's smart,
Yet did her paléd face disclose the passions of her heart.
Her sighing every hour, her weeping everywhere,   1785
Her reckless heed of meat, of sleep, and wearing of her gear,
The careful mother marks; then of her health afraid,
Because the griefs increaséd still, thus to her child she said:
   'Dear daughter, if you should long languish in this sort,
I stand in doubt that oversoon your sorrows will make short
Your loving father's life and mine, that love you more   [fore
Than our own proper breath and life. Bridle henceforth there-

Your grief and pain, yourself on joy your thought to set,
For time it is that now you should our Tybalt's death forget.
Of whom since God hath claimed the life that was but lent,
He is in bliss, ne is there cause why you should thus lament.
You can not call him back with tears and shriekings shrill:
It is a fault thus still to grudge at God's appointed will.'
The seely soul had now no longer power to feign,
No longer could she hide her harm, but answered thus again,
With heavy broken sighs, with visage pale and dead: 1801
   'Madam, the last of Tybalt's tears a great while since I
Whose spring hath been ere this so laded out by me, [shed;
That empty quite and moistureless I guess it now to be.
So that my painéd heart by conduits of the eyne   [brine.'
No more henceforth, as wont it was, shall gush forth dropping
The woeful mother knew not what her daughter meant,
And loth to vex her child by words, her peace she warely hent.
But when from hour to hour, from morrow to the morrow,
Still more and more she saw increased her daughter's wonted
      sorrow,   1810
All means she sought of her and household folk to know
The certain root whereon her grief and bootless moan doth
But lo, she hath in vain her time and labour lore,   [grow.
Wherefore without all measure is her heart tormented sore.
And sith herself could not find out the cause of care,
She thought it good to tell the sire how ill his child did fare.
And when she saw her time, thus to her fere she said:
   'Sir, if you mark our daughter well, the countenance of
     the maid,   1818

And how she fareth since that Tybalt unto death,
Before his time, forced by his foe, did yield his living breath,
Her face shall seem so changed, her doings eke so strange,
That you will greatly wonder at so great and sudden change.
Not only she forbears her meat, her drink, and sleep,
But now she tendeth nothing else but to lament and weep.
No greater joy hath she, nothing contents her heart
So much as in the chamber close to shut herself apart;
Where she doth so torment her poor afflicted mind,   1825
That much in danger stands her life, except some help we find.
But, out, alas, I see not how it may be found,   [abound.
Unless that first we might find whence her sorrows thus
For though with busy care I have employed my wit,   1831
And uséd all the ways I knew to learn the truth of it,
Neither extremity ne gentle means could boot;
She hideth close within her breast her secret sorrow's root.
This was my first conceit, that all her ruth arose   1835
Out of her cousin Tybalt's death, late slain of deadly foes;
But now my heart doth hold a new repugnant thought;
Some greater thing, not Tybalt's death, this change in her
Herself assuréd me that many days ago   [hath wrought.
She shed the last of Tybalt's tears; which word amazed me so
That I then could not guess what thing else might her grieve;
But now at length I have bethought me; and I do believe
The only crop and root of all my daughter's pain
Is grudging envy's faint disease: perhaps she doth disdain
To see in wedlock yoke the most part of her feres,   1845
Whilst only she unmarriéd doth lose so many years.

And more perchance she thinks you mind to keep her so;
Wherefore despairing doth she wear herself away with woe.
Therefore, dear sir, in time take on your daughter ruth;
For why, a brickle thing is glass, and frail is frailless youth.
Join her at once to some in link of marriage,   1851
That may be meet for our degree, and much about her age:
So shall you banish care out of your daughter's breast,
So we her parents, in our age, shall live in quiet rest.'
Whereto 'gan easily her husband to agree,   [he:
And to the mother's skilful talk thus straightway answered
   'Oft have I thought, dear wife, of all these things ere this,
But evermore my mind me gave, it should not be amiss
By farther leisure had a husband to provide;
Scarce saw she yet full sixteen years: too young to be a bride!
But since her state doth stand on terms so perilous,   1861
And that a maiden daughter is a treasure dangerous,
With so great speed I will endeavour to procure
A husband for our daughter young, her sickness faint to cure,
That you shall rest content, so warely will I choose,   1865
And she recover soon enough the time she seems to lose.
The whilst seek you to learn, if she in any part
Already hath, unware to us, fixéd her friendly heart;
Lest we have more respect to honour and to wealth,
Than to our daughter's quiet life, and to her happy health;
Whom I do hold as dear as th' apple of mine eye,   1871
And rather wish in poor estate and daughterless to die,
Than leave my goods and her y-thralled to such a one,[moan.'
Whose churlish dealing, I once dead, should be her cause of

This pleasant answer heard, the lady parts again, 1875
And Capulet, the maiden's sire, within a day or twain,
Conferreth with his friends for marriage of his daughter,
And many gentlemen there were with busy care that sought
Both for the maiden was well shapéd, young, and fair, [her;
As also well brought up, and wise; her father's only heir.
Among the rest was one inflamed with her desire, 1881
Who County Paris clepéd was; an earl he had to sire.
Of all the suitors him the father liketh best,
And easily unto the earl he maketh his behest,
Both of his own good will, and of his friendly aid, 1885
To win his wife unto his will, and to persuade the maid.
The wife did joy to hear the joyful husband say [day;
How happy hap, how meet a match, he had found out that
Ne did she seek to hide her joys within her heart,
But straight she hieth to Juliet; to her she tells, apart,
What happy talk, by mean of her, was past no rather 1891
Between the wooing Paris and her careful, loving father.
The person of the man, the features of his face, [grace,
His youthful years, his fairness, and his port, and seemly
With curious words she paints before her daughter's eyes, [skies.
And then with store of virtue's praise she heaves him to the
She vaunts his race, and gifts that Fortune did him give,
Whereby, she saith, both she and hers in great delight shall
When Juliet conceived her parents' whole intent, [live.
Whereto both love and reason's right forbode her to assent,
Within herself she thought, rather than be forsworn, 1901
With horses wild her tender parts asunder should be torn.

Not now, with bashful brow, in wonted wise, she spake,
But with unwonted boldness straight into these words she
    brake :
  'Madam, I marvel much that you so lavas are
Of me your child, your jewel once, your only joy and care,
As thus to yield me up at pleasure of another,
Before you know if I do like or else mislike my lover.
Do what you list, but yet of this assure you still,
If you do as you say you will, I yield not there until. 1910
For had I choice of twain, far rather would I choose
My part of all your goods and eke my breath and life to lose,
Than grant that he possess of me the smallest part ;
First, weary of my painful life, my cares shall kill my heart,
Else will I pierce my breast with sharp and bloody knife ;
And you, my mother, shall become the murd'ress of my life,
In giving me to him whom I ne can, ne may,   1917
Ne ought, to love : wherefore on knees, dear mother, I you
To let me live henceforth, as I have lived tofore ;   [pray,
Cease all your troubles for my sake, and care for me no more ;
But suffer Fortune fierce to work on me her will,   1921
In her it lieth to do me boot, in her it lieth to spill.
For whilst you for the best desire to place me so,
You haste away my ling'ring death, and double all my woe.
  So deep this answer made the sorrows down to sink
Into the mother's breast, that she ne knoweth what to think
Of these her daughter's words, but all appalled she stands,
And up unto the heavens she throws her wond'ring head
    and hands.   1928

And, nigh beside herself, her husband hath she sought;
She tells him all; she doth forget ne yet she hideth aught.
The testy old man, wroth, disdainful without measure,
Sends forth his folk in haste for her, and bids them take no
Ne on her tears or plaint at all to have remorse,   [leisure:
But, if they cannot with her will, to bring the maid perforce.
The message heard, they part, to fetch that they must fet,
And willingly with them walks forth obedient Juliet.   1936
Arrivéd in the place, when she her father saw,
Of whom, as much as duty would, the daughter stood in awe,
The servants sent away, (the mother thought it meet,)
The woeful daughter all bewept fell grovelling at his feet,
Which she doth wash with tears as she thus grovelling lies—
So fast, and eke so plenteously distil they from her eyes:
When she to call for grace her mouth doth think to open,
Muët she is—for sighs and sobs her fearful talk have broken.
    The sire, whose swelling wrath her tears could not assuage,
With fiery eyne, and scarlet cheeks, thus spake her in his rage,
Whilst ruthfully stood by the maiden's mother mild: 1947
    'Listen,' quoth he, 'unthankful and thou disobedient child,
Hast thou so soon let slip out of thy mind the word
That thou so oftentimes hast heard rehearséd at my board?
How much the Roman youth of parents stood in awe,
And eke what power upon their seed the fathers had by
Whom they not only might pledge, alienate, and sell,   [law?
Whenso they stood in need, but more, if children did rebel,
The parents had the power of life and sudden death.   1955
What if those goodmen should again receive the living breath,

In how strait bonds would they thy stubborn body bind?
What weapons would they seek for thee? what torments
    would they find?
To chasten, if they saw, the lewdness of thy life,
Thy great unthankfulness to me, and shameful sturdy strife?
Such care thy mother had, so dear thou wert to me,　　1961
That I with long and earnest suit provided have for thee
One of the greatest lords that wones about this town,
And for his many virtues' sake a man of great renown.
Of whom both thou and I unworthy are too much,　　1965
So rich ere long he shall be left, his father's wealth is such,
Such is the nobleness and honour of the race　　　　[case
From whence his father came: and yet, thou playest in this
The dainty fool, and stubborn girl; for want of skill　1969
Thou dost refuse thy offered weal, and disobey my will.
Even by His strength I swear, that first did give me life,
And gave me in my youth the strength to get thee on my
Unless by Wednesday next thou bend as I am bent,　[wife,
And at our castle called Freetown thou freely do assent
To County Paris' suit, and promise to agree　　　　1975
To whatsoever then shall pass 'twixt him, my wife, and me,
Not only will I give all that I have away
From thee, to those that shall me love, me honour, and obey,
But also to so close and to so hard a gaol
I shall thee wed, for all thy life, that sure thou shalt not fail
A thousand times a day to wish for sudden death,　　1981
And curse the day and hour when first thy lungs did give
    thee breath.

Advise thee well, and say that thou art warnéd now,
And think not that I speak in sport, or mind to break my vow.
For were it not that I to County Paris gave   1985
My faith, which I must keep unfalsed, my honour so to save,
Ere thou go hence, myself would see thee chastened so, [know ;
That thou should'st once for all be taught thy duty how to
And what revenge of old the angry sires did find   [kind.'
Against their children that rebelled and showed themself un-
    These said, the old man straight is gone in haste away,
Ne for his daughter's answer would the testy father stay.
And after him his wife doth follow out of door,   [floor :
And there they leave their chidden child kneeling upon the
Then she that oft had seen the fury of her sire,   1995
Dreading what might come of his rage, nould farther stir his
Unto her chamber she withdrew herself apart,   [ire.
Where she was wonted to unload the sorrows of her heart.
There did she not so much busy her eyes in sleeping,
As overpressed with restless thoughts in piteous bootless weep-
The fast falling of tears make not her tears decrease,   [ing.
Ne, by the pouring forth of plaint, the cause of plaint doth
So that to th' end the moan and sorrow may decay,   [cease.
The best is that she seek some mean to take the cause away.
Her weary bed betime the woeful wight forsakes,   2005
And to Saint Francis' church to mass her way devoutly takes.
The friar forth is called ; she prays him hear her shrift ;
Devotion is in so young years a rare and precious gift.
When on her tender knees the dainty lady kneels,
In mind to pour forth all the grief that inwardly she feels,

With sighs and salted tears her shriving doth begin,   2011
For she of heapéd sorrows hath to speak, <u>and not of sin.</u>
Her voice with piteous plaint was made already hoarse,
And hasty sobs, when she would speak, brake off her words per-
But as she may, piece-meal, she poureth in his lap   [force.
The marriage news, a mischief new, preparéd by mishap,
Her parents' promise erst to County Paris past,
Her father's threats she telleth him, and thus concludes at last:
'Once was I wedded well, ne will I wed again;
For since I know I may not be the wedded wife of twain,
For I am bound to have one God, one faith, one make,   2021
My purpose is as soon as I shall hence my journey take,
With these two hands, which joined unto the heavens I stretch,
The hasty death which I desire, unto myself to reach.
This day, O Romeus, this day thy woeful wife   2025
Will bring the end of all her cares by ending careful life.
So my departed sprite shall witness to the sky,
And eke my blood unto the earth bear record, how that I
Have kept my faith unbroke, steadfast unto my friend.'

When this her heavy tale was told, her vow eke at an end,
Her gazing here and there, her fierce and staring look,
Did witness that some lewd attempt her heart had undertook.
Whereat the friar astound, and ghastfully afraid   2033
Lest she by deed perform her word, thus much to her he said:
'Ah, Lady Juliet, what need the words you spake?
I pray you, grant me one request, for blesséd Mary's sake.
Measure somewhat your grief, hold here awhile your peace;
Whilst I bethink me of your case, your plaint and sorrows cease.

Such comfort will I give you, ere you part from hence,
And for th'assaults of Fortune's ire prepare so sure defence,
So wholesome salve will I for your afflictions find,   2041
That you shall hence depart again with well contented mind.'

   His words have chaséd straight out of her heart despair,
Her black and ugly dreadful thoughts by hope are waxen fair.
So Friar Laurence now hath left her there alone,   2045
And he out of the church in haste is to his chamber gone;
Where sundry thoughts within his careful head arise;
The old man's foresight divers doubts hath set before his eyes,
His conscience one while condemns it for a sin
To let her take Paris to spouse, since he himself had bin
The chiefest cause, that she unknown to father or mother,
Not five months past, in that self place was wedded to another.
Another while an hugy heap of dangers dread
His restless thought hath heapéd up within his troubled head.
Even of itself th'attempt he judgeth perilous;   2055
The execution eke he deems so much more dangerous,
That to a woman's grace he must himself commit,
That young is, simple and unware, for weighty affairs unfit;
For if she fail in aught, the matter publishéd,
Both she and Romeus were undone, himself eke punishéd.
When to and fro in mind he divers thoughts had cast, 2061
With tender pity and with ruth his heart was won at last;
He thought he rather would in hazard set his fame,
Than suffer such adultery.   Resolving on the same,
Out of his closet straight he took a little glass,   2065
And then with double haste returned where woeful Juliet was;

Whom he hath found well-nigh in trance, scarce drawing
Attending still to hear the news of life or else of death. [breath,
Of whom he did enquire of the appointed day:
   'On Wednesday next,' quod Juliet, 'so doth my father say,
I must give my consent; but, as I do remember,   2071
The solemn day of marriage is the tenth day of September.'
   'Dear daughter,' quoth the friar, 'of good cheer see thou be,
For lo, Saint Francis of his grace hath showed a way to me,
By which I may both thee and Romeus together   2075
Out of the bondage which you fear assurédly deliver.
Even from the holy font thy husband have I known,
And, since he grew in years, have kept his counsels as mine
For from his youth he would unfold to me his heart, [own.
And often have I curéd him of anguish and of smart; 2080
I know that by desert his friendship I have won,
And I him hold as dear as if he were my proper son.
Wherefore my friendly heart cannot abide that he
Should wrongfully in aught be harmed, if that it lay in me
To right or to revenge the wrong by my advice,   2085
Or timely to prevent the same in any other wise.
And sith thou art his wife, thee am I bound to love,
For Romeus' friendship's sake, and seek thy anguish to remove,
And dreadful torments, which thy heart besiegen round;
Wherefore, my daughter, give good ear unto my counsels sound.
Forget not what I say, ne tell it any wight,   2091
Not to the nurse thou trustest so, as Romeus is thy knight;
For on this thread doth hang thy death and eke thy life,
My fame or shame, his weal or woe that chose thee to his wife.

Thou art not ignorant—because of such renown   2095
As everywhere is spread of me, but chiefly in this town—
That in my youthful days abroad I travelléd,
Through every land found out by men, by men inhabited;
So twenty years from home, in lands unknown a guest,
I never gave my weary limbs long time of quiet rest,   2100
But in the desert woods, to beasts of cruel kind,
Or on the seas to drenching waves, at pleasure of the wind,
I have committed them, to ruth of rover's hand,
And to a thousand dangers more, by water and by land.
But not in vain, my child, hath all my wand'ring bin;
Beside the great contentedness my sprite abideth in,   2106
That by the pleasant thought of passéd things doth grow,
One private fruit more have I plucked, which thou shalt
        shortly know:
What force the stones, the plants, and metals have to work,
And divers other things that in the bowels of earth do lurk,
With care I have sought out, with pain I did them prove;
With them eke can I help myself at times of my behove,—
Although the science be against the laws of men,—
When sudden danger forceth me; but yet most chiefly when
The work to do is least displeasing unto God,   2115
Not helping to do any sin that wreakful Jove forbode.
For since in life no hope of long abode I have,
But now am come unto the brink of my appointed grave,
And that my death draws near, whose stripe I may not
        shun,   2119
But shall be called to make account of all that I have done,

Now ought I from henceforth more deeply print in mind
The judgment of the Lord, than when youth's folly made me
When love and fond desire were boiling in my breast, [blind,
Whence hope and dread by striving thoughts had banished
    friendly rest.   2124
Know therefore, daughter, that with other gifts which I
Have well attainéd to, by grace and favour of the sky,
Long since I did find out, and yet the way I know
Of certain roots and savoury herbs to make a kind of dough,
Which bakéd hard, and beat into a powder fine,
And drunk with conduit water, or with any kind of wine,
It doth in half an hour astonne the taker so,   2131
And mast'reth all his senses, that he feeleth weal nor woe:
And so it burieth up the sprite and living breath,
That even the skilful leech would say, that he is slain by
    death.
One virtue more it hath, as marvellous as this;   2135
The taker, by receiving it, at all not grievéd is;
But painless as a man that thinketh nought at all,
Into a sweet and quiet sleep immediately doth fall;
From which, according to the quantity he taketh,
Longer or shorter is the time before the sleeper waketh;
And thence, th'effect once wrought, again it doth restore
Him that received unto the state wherein he was before.
Wherefore, mark well the end of this my tale begun,   2143
And thereby learn what is by thee hereafter to be done.
Cast off from thee at once the weed of womanish dread,
With manly courage arm thyself from heel unto the head;

For only on the fear or boldness of thy breast
The happy hap or ill mishap of thy affair doth rest.
Receive this vial small and keep it as thine eye;   2149
And on thy marriage day, before the sun do clear the sky,
Fill it with water full up to the very brim,   [and limb
Then drink it off, and thou shalt feel throughout each vein
A pleasant slumber slide, and quite dispread at length
On all thy parts, from every part reave all thy kindly strength;
Withouten moving thus thy idle parts shall rest,   2155
No pulse shall go, ne heart once beat within thy hollow breast,
But thou shalt lie as she that dieth in a trance: [chance;
Thy kinsmen and thy trusty friends shall wail the sudden
Thy corpse then will they bring to grave in this churchyard,
Where thy forefathers long ago a costly tomb prepared,
Both for themself and eke for those that should come after,
Both deep it is, and long and large, where thou shalt rest, my
Till I to Mantua send for Romeus, thy knight; [daughter,
Out of the tomb both he and I will take thee forth that night.
And when out of thy sleep thou shalt awake again,   2165
Then may'st thou go with him from hence; and, healéd of thy
In Mantua lead with him unknown a pleasant life; [pain,
And yet perhaps in time to come, when cease shall all the strife,
And that the peace is made 'twixt Romeus and his foes,
Myself may find so fit a time these secrets to disclose, 2170
Both to my praise, and to thy tender parents' joy,
That dangerless, without reproach, thou shalt thy love enjoy.'

When of his skilful tale the friar had made an end,
To which our Juliet so well her ear and wits did bend,

That she hath heard it all and hath forgotten nought, 2175
Her fainting heart was comforted with hope and pleasant
And then to him she said : 'Doubt not but that I will [thought,
With stout and unappalléd heart your happy hest fulfil.
Yea, if I wist it were a venomous deadly drink, [should sink,
Rather would I that through my throat the certain bane
Than I, not drinking it, into his hands should fall, 2181
That hath no part of me as yet, ne ought to have at all.
Much more I ought with bold and with a willing heart
To greatest danger yield myself, and to the deadly smart,
To come to him on whom my life doth wholly stay, 2185
That is my only heart's delight, and so he shall be aye.'
'Then go,' quoth he, 'my child, I pray that God on high
Direct thy foot, and by thy hand upon the way thee guie.
God grant he so confirm in thee thy present will,
That no inconstant toy thee let thy promise to fulfil.' 2190
A thousand thanks and more our Juliet gave the friar,
And homeward to her father's house joyful she doth retire ;
And as with stately gait she passéd through the street,
She saw her mother in the door, that with her there would
In mind to ask if she her purpose yet did hold, [meet,
In mind also, apart 'twixt them, her duty to have told ;
Wherefore with pleasant face, and with unwonted cheer,
As soon as she was unto her approachéd somewhat near,
Before the mother spake, thus did she first begin : 2199
' Madam, at Saint Francis' church have I this morning bin,
Where I did make abode a longer while, percase,
Than duty would ; yet have I not been absent from this place

G

So long a while, without a great and just cause why;
This fruit have I receivéd there—my heart, erst like to die,
Is now revived again, and my afflicted breast,   2205
Releaséd from affliction, restoréd is to rest!
For lo, my troubled ghost, alas, too sore dis-eased,
By ghostly counsel and advice hath Friar Laurence eased;
To whom I did at large discourse my former life,
x And in confession did I tell of all our passéd strife;   2210
Of County Paris' suit, and how my lord, my sire,
By my ungrate and stubborn strife I stirréd unto ire;
But lo, the holy friar hath by his ghostly lore
Made me another woman now than I had been before.
By strength of arguments he chargéd so my mind, [could find.
That, though I sought, no sure defence my searching thought
So forced I was at length to yield up witless will,
And promised to be ordered by the friar's praiséd skill.
Wherefore, albeit I had rashly, long before,
The bed and rites of marriage for many years forswore,
Yet mother, now behold your daughter at your will, 2221
Ready, if you command her aught, your pleasure to fulfil.
Wherefore in humble wise, dear madam, I you pray,
To go unto my lord and sire, withouten long delay;
Of him first pardon crave of faults already past,   2225
And show him, if it pleaseth you, his child is now at last
Obedient to his just and to his skilful hest,   [prest
And that I will, God lending life, on Wednesday next be
To wait on him and you, unto th' appointed place,
Where I will, in your hearing, and before my father's face,

Unto the County give my faith and whole assent,   2231
And take him for my lord and spouse; thus fully am I bent;
And that out of your mind I may remove all doubt,
Unto my closet fare I now, to search and to choose out
The bravest garments and the richest jewels there,   [wear;
Which, better him to please, I mind on Wednesday next to
For if I did excel the famous Grecian rape,
Yet might attire help to amend my beauty and my shape.'
     The simple mother was rapt into great delight;   2239
Not half a word could she bring forth, but in this joyful plight
With nimble foot she ran, and with unwonted pace,
Unto her pensive husband, and to him with pleasant face
She told what she had heard, and praiseth much the friar;
And joyful tears ran down the cheeks of this gray-bearded sire.
With hands and eyes heaved up he thanks God in his heart,
And then he saith : ' This is not, wife, the friar's first desert;
Oft hath he showed to us great friendship heretofore, 2247
By helping us at needful times with wisdom's precious lore.
In all our commonweal scarce one is to be found
But is, for some good turn, unto this holy father bound.
Oh that the third part of my goods—I do not feign— 2251
But twenty of his passéd years might purchase him again!
So much in recompense of friendship would I give,
So much, in faith, his extreme age my friendly heart doth
     grieve.'
     These said, the glad old man from home go'th straight
     abroad,
                                                          2255
And to the stately palace hieth where Paris made abode;

Whom he desires to be on Wednesday next his geast,
At Freetown, where he minds to make for him a costly feast.
But lo, the earl saith, such feasting were but lost,
And counsels him till marriage-time to spare so great a cost,
For then he knoweth well the charges will be great ; 2261
The whilst, his heart desireth still her sight, and not his meat.
He craves of Capulet that he may straight go see
Fair Juliet ; whereto he doth right willingly agree.
The mother, warned before, her daughter doth prepare ;
She warneth and she chargeth her that in no wise she spare
Her courteous speech, her pleasant looks, and comely grace,
But liberally to give them forth when Paris comes in place :
Which she as cunningly could set forth to the show,
As cunning craftsmen to the sale do set their wares on row ;
That ere the County did out of her sight depart,   2271
So secretly unwares to him she stale away his heart,
That of his life and death the wily wench had power.
And now his longing heart thinks long for their appointed
And with importune suit the parents doth he pray   [hour,
The wedlock knot to knit soon up, and haste the marriage day.
  The wooer hath passed forth the first day in this sort,
And many other more than this, in pleasure and disport.
At length the wishéd time of long hopéd delight,   [plight.
As Paris thought, drew near ; but near approachéd heavy
Against the bridal day the parents did prepare   2281
Such rich attire, such furniture, such store of dainty fare,
That they which did behold the same the night before
Did think and say, a man could scarcely wish for any more.

Nothing did seem too dear; the dearest things were bought;
And, as the written story saith, indeed there wanted nought
That 'longed to his degree, and honour of his stock; 2287
But Juliet, the whilst, her thoughts within her breast did lock;
Even from the trusty nurse, whose secretness was tried,
The secret counsel of her heart the nurse-child seeks to hide.
For sith, to mock her Dame, she did not stick to lie, 2291
She thought no sin with show of truth to blear her nurse's
In chamber secretly the tale she 'gan renew,   [eye.
That at the door she told her dame, as though it had been
The flatt'ring nurse did praise the friar for his skill, [true.
And said that she had done right well by wit to order will.
She setteth forth at large the father's furious rage, 2297
And eke she praiseth much to her the second marriage;
And County Paris now she praiseth ten times more, [before.
By wrong, than she herself, by right, had Romeus praised
Paris shall dwell there still, Romeus shall not return; 2301
What shall it boot her life to languish still and mourn?
The pleasures past before she must account as gain;
But if he do return, what then?—for one she shall have twain.
The one shall use her as his lawful wedded wife, 2305
In wanton love with equal joy the other lead his life;
And best shall she be sped of any townish dame,
Of husband and of paramour to find her change of game.
These words and like the nurse did speak, in hope to please,
But greatly did these wicked words the lady's mind dis-ease;
But aye she hid her wrath, and seeméd well content, 2311
When daily did the naughty nurse new arguments invent.

But when the bride perceived her hour approachéd near,
She sought, the best she could, to feign, and tempered so her
That by her outward look no living wight could guess [cheer,
Her inward woe; and yet anew renewed is her distress.
Unto her chamber doth the pensive wight repair,   [stair.
And in her hand a percher light the nurse bears up the
In Juliet's chamber was her wonted use to lie;   [descry,
Wherefore her mistress, dreading that she should her work
As soon as she began her pallet to unfold,   2321
Thinking to lie that night where she was wont to lie of old,
Doth gently pray her seek her lodging somewhere else;
And, lest she, crafty, should suspect, a ready reason tells.
'Dear friend,' quoth she, 'you know to-morrow is the day
Of new contràct; wherefore, this night, my purpose is to pray
Unto the heavenly minds that dwell above the skies,
And order all the course of things as they can best devise,
That they so smile upon the doings of to-morrow,
That all the remnant of my life may be exempt from sorrow :
Wherefore, I pray you, leave me here alone this night, 2331
But see that you to-morrow come before the dawning light,
For you must curl my hair, and set on my attire.'
And easily the loving nurse did yield to her desire,
For she within her head did cast before no doubt;   2335
She little knew the close attempt her nurse-child went about.
   The nurse departed once, the chamber door shut close,
Assuréd that no living wight her doing might disclose,
She pouréd forth into the vial of the friar
Water, out of a silver ewer that on the board stood by her.

The sleepy mixture made, fair Juliet doth it hide   2341
Under her bolster soft, and so unto her bed she hied:
Where divers novel thoughts arise within her head,
And she is so environéd about with deadly dread,
That what before she had resolved undoubtedly   2345
That same she calleth into doubt; and lying doubtfully,
Whilst honest love did strive with dread of deadly pain,
With hands y-wrung, and weeping eyes, thus gan she to com-
'What, is there any one, beneath the heavens high, [plain :—
So much unfortunate as I? so much past hope as I?   2350
What, am I not myself, of all that yet were born,   [scorn?
The deepest drenchéd in despair, and most in Fortune's
For lo, the world for me hath nothing else to find,
Beside mishap and wretchedness and anguish of the mind;
Since that the cruel cause of my unhappiness   [distress,
Hath put me to this sudden plunge, and brought to such
As, to the end I may my name and conscience save,   2357
I must devour the mixéd drink that by me here I have,
Whose working and whose force as yet I do not know.'
And of this piteous plaint began another doubt to grow:
'What do I know,' quoth she, 'if that this powder shall
Sooner or later than it should, or else, not work at all? 2362
And then my craft descried as open as the day,
The people's tale and laughing-stock shall I remain for aye.'
'And what know I,' quoth she, 'if serpents odious,
And other beasts and worms that are of nature venomous,
That wonted are to lurk in dark caves underground, [found,
And commonly, as I have heard, in dead men's tombs are

Shall harm me, yea or nay, where I shall lie as dead?——
Or how shall I that alway have in so fresh air been bred,
Endure the lothsome stink of such an heapéd store   2371
Of carcases not yet consumed, and bones that long before
Intombéd were, where I my sleeping-place shall have,
Where all my ancestors do rest, my kindred's common grave?
Shall not the friar and my Romeus, when they come,
Find me, if I awake before, y-stifled in the tomb?'   2376
   And whilst she in these thoughts doth dwell somewhat too
The force of her imagining anon did wax so strong,   [long,
That she surmised she saw, out of the hollow vault,
A grisly thing to look upon, the carcase of Tybalt;   2380
Right in the selfsame sort that she few days before   [sore.
Had seen him in his blood embrued, to death eke wounded
And then when she again within herself had weighed
That quick she should be buried there, and by his side be laid,
All comfortless, for she shall living fere have none,   2385
But many a rotten carcase, and full many a naked bone;
Her dainty tender parts 'gan shiver all for dread,
Her golden hairs did stand upright upon her chillish head.
Then presséd with the fear that she there livéd in,   [skin,
A sweat as cold as mountain ice pierced through her slender
That with the moisture hath wet every part of hers: 2391
And more besides, she vainly thinks, whilst vainly thus she
A thousand bodies dead have compassed her about,   [fears,
And lest they will dismember her she greatly stands in doubt.
But when she felt her strength began to wear away,   2395
By little and little, and in her heart her fear increaséd aye,

Dreading that weakness might, or foolish cowardice,
Hinder the execution of the purposed enterprise,
As she had frantic been, in haste the glass she caught,
And up she drank the mixture quite, withouten farther
    thought.
Then on her breast she crossed her arms long and small,
And so, her senses failing her, into a trance did fall. 2402
    And when that Phœbus bright heaved up his seemly head,
And from the East in open skies his glist'ring rays dispread,
The nurse unshut the door, for she the key did keep,
And doubting she had slept too long, she thought to break her
    sleep ;
First softly did she call, then louder thus did cry :
' Lady, you sleep too long ; the earl will raise you by and by.'
But, well away, in vain unto the deaf she calls,
She thinks to speak to Juliet, but speaketh to the walls.
If all the dreadful noise that might on earth be found, 2411
Or on the roaring seas, or if the dreadful thunder's sound
Had blown into her ears, I think they could not make
The sleeping wight before the time by any means awake ;
So were the sprites of life shut up, and senses thralled ;
Wherewith the seely careful nurse was wondrously appalled.
She thought to daw her now as she had done of old, [cold ;
But lo, she found her parts were stiff and more than marble
Neither at mouth nor nose found she recourse of breath ;
Two certain arguments were these of her untimely death.
Wherefore, as one distraught, she to her mother ran, [can,
With scratchéd face, and hair betorn, but no word speak she

At last, with much ado, 'Dead,' quoth she, 'is my child!'
'Now, out, alas!' the mother cried, and as a tiger wild, 2424
Whose whelps, whilst she is gone out of her den to prey,
The hunter greedy of his game doth kill or carry away;
So raging forth she ran unto her Juliet's bed,
And there she found her darling and her only comfort dead.
  Then shrieked she out as loud as serve her would her breath,
And then, that pity was to hear, thus cried she out on Death:
'Ah cruel Death,' quoth she, 'that thus against all right,
Hast ended my felicity, and robbed my heart's delight,
Do now thy worst to me, once wreak thy wrath for all,
Even in despite I cry to thee, thy vengeance let thou fall.
Whereto stay I, alas, since Juliet is gone?   2435
Whereto live I, since she is dead, except to wail and moan?
Alack, dear child, my tears for thee shall never cease;
Even as my days of life increase, so shall my plaint increase:
Such store of sorrow shall afflict my tender heart,
That deadly pangs, when they assail shall not augment my
    smart.'
Then 'gan she so to sob, it seemed her heart would brast;
And while she crieth thus, behold, the father at the last,
The County Paris, and of gentlemen a rout,
And ladies of Verona town and country round about,
Both kindreds and allies thither apace have preast,   2445
For by their presence there they sought to honour so the feast;
But when the heavy news the bidden guests did hear,
So much they mourned, that who had seen their count'nance
    and their cheer,

Might easily have judged by that that they had seen,
That day the day of wrath and eke of pity to have been.
But more than all the rest the father's heart was so 2451
Smit with the heavy news, and so shut up with sudden woe,
That he ne had the power his daughter to be-weep, [keep.
Ne yet to speak, but long is forced his tears and plaint to
In all the haste he hath for skilful leeches sent; 2455
And, hearing of her passéd life, they judge with one assent
The cause of this her death was inward care and thought;
And then with double force again the doubled sorrows
If ever there hath been a lamentable day, [wrought.
A day ruthful, unfortunate and fatal, then I say, 2460
The same was it in which through Verone town was spread
The woeful news how Juliet was stervéd in her bed.
For so she was bemoaned both of the young and old,
That it might seem to him that would the common plaint
That all the commonwealth did stand in jeopardy; [behold,
So universal was the plaint, so piteous was the cry. 2466
For lo, beside her shape and native beauty's hue,
With which, like as she grew in age, her virtues' praises
She was also so wise, so lowly, and so mild, [grew,
That even from the hoary head unto the witless child, 2470
She wan the hearts of all, so that there was not one,
Ne great, ne small, but did that day her wretched state bemoan.
  Whilst Juliet slept, and whilst the other weepen thus,
Our Friar Laurence hath by this sent one to Romeus,
A friar of his house,—there never was a better, 2475
He trusted him even as himself,—to whom he gave a letter,

In which he written had of everything at length, [strength ;
That passed 'twixt Juliet and him, and of the powder's
The next night after that, he willeth him to come
To help to take his Juliet out of the hollow tomb,   2480
For by that time the drink, he saith, will cease to work,
And for one night his wife and he within his cell shall lurk ;
Then shall he carry her to Mantua away,—
Till fickle Fortune favour him,—disguised in man's array.
  This letter closed he sends to Romeus by his brother ;
He chargeth him that in no case he give it any other. 2486
Apace our Friar John to Mantua him hies ;
And, for because in Italy it is a wonted guise
That friars in the town should seldom walk alone,
But of their convent aye should be accompanied with one
Of his profession, straight a house he findeth out,   2491
In mind to take some friar with him, to walk the town about.
But entered once he might not issue out again,
For that a brother of the house, a day before or twain, [hate—
Died of the plague—a sickness which they greatly fear and
So were the brethren charged to keep within their convent
Barred of their fellowship that in the town do wone ;   [gate,
The townfolk eke commanded are the friar's house to shun,
Till they that had the care of health their freedom should
     renew ;
Whereof, as you shall shortly hear, a mischief great there
     grew.   2500
The friar by this restraint, beset with dread and sorrow,
Not knowing what the letters held, deferred until the morrow ;

And then he thought in time to send to Romeus.   [thus,
But whilst at Mantua where he was, these doings framéd
The town of Juliet's birth was wholly busiéd   2505
About her obsequies, to see their darling buriéd.
Now is the parents' mirth quite changéd into moan,
And now to sorrow is returned the joy of every one ; [change,
And now the wedding weeds for mourning weeds they
And Hymenë into a dirge ;—alas ! it seemeth strange : 2510
Instead of marriage gloves, now funeral gloves they have,
And whom they should see marriéd, they follow to the grave.
The feast that should have been of pleasure and of joy,
Hath every dish and cup filled full of sorrow and annoy.
    Now throughout Italy this common use they have, 2515
That all the best of every stock are earthéd in one grave :
For every household, if it be of any fame,   [name ;
Doth build a tomb, or dig a vault, that bears the household's
Wherein, if any of that kindred hap to die,
They are bestowed ; else in the same no other corpse may lie.
The Capulets her corpse in such a one did lay,   2521
Where Tybalt, slain of Romeus, was laid the other day.ᴵ
Another use there is, that whosoever dies,
Borne to their church with open face upon the bier he lies,
In wonted weed attired, not wrapped in winding sheet.
So, as by chance he walked abroad, our Romeus' man did meet
His master's wife ; the sight with sorrow straight did wound
His honest heart ; with tears he saw her lodgéd underground.
And, for he had been sent to Verone for a spy,
The doings of the Capulets by wisdom to descry,   2530

And for he knew her death did touch his master most,
Alas, too soon, with heavy news he hied away in post;
And in his house he found his master Romeus,
Where he, besprent with many tears, began to speak him thus :
  'Sire, unto you of late is chanced so great a harm,   2535
That sure, except with constancy you seek yourself to arm,
I fear that straight you will breathe out your latter breath,
And I, most wretched wight, shall be th'occasion of your death.
Know, sir, that yesterday, my lady and your wife,
I wot not by what sudden grief, hath made exchange of life;
And for because on earth she found nought but unrest,   2541
In heaven hath she sought to find a place of quiet rest;
And with these weeping eyes myself have seen her laid
Within the tomb of Capulets' : and herewithal he stayed.
  This sudden message' sound, sent forth with sighs and tears,
Our Romeus received too soon with open list'ning ears;
And thereby hath sunk in such sorrow in his heart,
That lo, his sprite annoyéd sore with torment and with smart,
Was like to break out of his prison house perforce,   [corse.
And that he might fly after hers, would leave the massy
But earnest love that will not fail him till his end,   2551
This fond and sudden fantasy into his head did send :
That if near unto her he offered up his breath,   [death.
That then a hundred thousand parts more glorious were his
Eke should his painful heart a great deal more be eased,
And more also, he vainly thought, his lady better pleased.
Wherefore when he his face hath washed with water clean,
Lest that the stains of driéd tears might on his cheeks be seen,

And so his sorrow should of everyone be spied,   2559
Which he with all his care did seek from everyone to hide,
Straight, weary of the house, he walketh forth abroad :
His servant, at the master's hest, in chamber still abode ;
And then fro street to street he wand'reth up and down,
To see if he in any place may find, in all the town,
A salve meet for his sore, an oil fit for his wound ;   [found.
And seeking long—alack, too soon !—the thing he sought, he
    An apothecary sat unbusied at his door,
Whom by his heavy countenance he guesséd to be poor.
And in his shop he saw his boxes were but few,
And in his window, of his wares, there was so small a shew ;
Wherefore our Romeus assuredly hath thought,   2571
What by no friendship could be got, with money should be
For needy lack is like the poor man to compel   [bought ;
To sell that which the city's law forbiddeth him to sell.
Then by the hand he drew the needy man apart,   2575
And with the sight of glitt'ring gold inflaméd hath his heart :
'Take fifty crowns of gold,' quoth he, 'I give them thee,
So that, before I part from hence, thou straight deliver me
Some poison strong, that may in less than half an hour
Kill him whose wretched hap shall be the potion to devour.'
The wretch by covetise is won, and doth assent   2581
To sell the thing, whose sale ere long, too late, he doth repent.
In haste he poison sought, and closely he it bound,
And then began with whispering voice thus in his ear to round :
'Fair sir,' quoth he, 'be sure this is the speeding gear, 2585
And more there is than you shall need ; for half of that is there

Will serve, I undertake, in less than half an hour
To kill the strongest man alive ; such is the poison's power.'
    Then Romeus, somewhat eased of one part of his care,
Within his bosom putteth up his dear unthrifty ware. 2590
Returning home again, he sent his man away
To Verone town, and chargeth him that he, without delay,
Provide both instruments to open wide the tomb,
And lights to show him Juliet ; and stay till he shall come
Near to the place whereas his loving wife doth rest,   2595
And chargeth him not to bewray the dolours of his breast.
Peter, these heard, his leave doth of his master take ;
Betime he comes to town, such haste the painful man did make :
And then with busy care he seeketh to fulfil,
But doth disclose unto no wight his woeful master's will.
Would God, he had herein broken his master's hest ! 2601
Would God, that to the friar he had discloséd all his breast !
But Romeus the while with many a deadly thought
Provokéd much, hath causéd ink and paper to be brought,
And in few lines he did of all his love discourse,   2605
How by the friar's help, and by the knowledge of the nurse,
The wedlock knot was knit, and by what mean that night
And many mo he did enjoy his happy heart's delight ;
Where he the poison bought, and how his life should end ;
And so his wailful tragedy the wretched man hath penned.
    The letters closed and sealed, directed to his sire,   2611
He locketh in his purse, and then a post-horse doth he hire.
When he approachéd near, he warely lighted down,
And even with the shade of night he entered Verone town ;

Where he hath found his man, waiting when he should come,
With lantern, and with instruments to open Juliet's tomb.
'Help, Peter, help,' quod he, 'help to remove the stone,
And straight when I am gone fro thee, my Juliet to bemoan,
See that thou get thee hence, and on the pain of death
I charge thee that thou come not near while I abide beneath,
Ne seek thou not to let thy master's enterprise,   2621
Which he hath fully purposéd to do, in any wise.
Take there a letter, which, as soon as he shall rise,
Present it in the morning to my loving father's eyes;
Which unto him, perhaps, far pleasanter shall seem,   2625
Than either I do mind to say, or thy gross head can deem.'
    Now Peter, that knew not the purpose of his heart,
Obediently a little way withdrew himself apart;
And then our Romeus (the vault-stone set upright),
Descended down, and in his hand he bare the candle light.
And then with piteous eye the body of his wife   2631
He 'gan behold, who surely was the organ of his life;
For whom unhappy now he is, but erst was blissed, [kissed;
He watered her with tears, and then a hundred times her
And in his folded arms full straitly he her plight,   2635
But no way could his greedy eyes be filléd with her sight:
His fearful hands he laid upon her stomach cold,
And them on divers parts beside the woeful wight did hold.
But when he could not find the signs of life he sought,
Out of his curséd box he drew the poison that he bought;
Whereof he greedily devoured the greater part,   [heart:
And then he cried, with deadly sigh fetched from his mourning

H

'O Juliet, of whom the world unworthy was,   [pass,
From which, for world's unworthiness thy worthy ghost did
What death more pleasant could my heart wish to abide
Than that which here it suff'reth now, so near thy friendly side?
Or else so glorious tomb how could my youth have craved,
As in one self-same vault with thee haply to be ingraved?
What epitaph more worth, or half so excellent,
To consecrate my memory, could any man invent,   2650
As this our mutual and our piteous sacrifice
Of life, set light for love?'
                                But while he talketh in this wise,
And thought as yet awhile his dolours to enforce,   [force;
His tender heart began to faint, pressed with the venom's
Which little and little 'gan to overcome his heart,   2655
And whilst his busy eyne he threw about to every part, ˉ
He saw, hard by the corse of sleeping Juliet,
Bold Tybalt's carcase dead, which was not all consuméd yet;
To whom, as having life, in this sort speaketh he:
    'Ah, cousin dear, Tybalt, whereso thy restless sprite now be,
With stretchéd hands to thee for mercy now I cry,   2661
For that before thy kindly hour I forcéd thee to die.
But if with quenchéd life not quenchéd be thine ire,
But with revenging lust as yet thy heart be set on fire,
What more amends, or cruel wreak desirest thou   [now?
To see on me, than this which here is showed forth to thee
Who reft by force of arms from thee thy living breath,
The same with his own hand, thou seest, doth poison him-
    self to death.

And for he causéd thee in tomb too soon to lie,
Too soon also, younger than thou, himself he layeth by.' 2670
 These said, when he 'gan feel the poison's force prevail,
And little and little mastered life for aye began to fail,
Kneeling upon his knees, he said with voice full low,—
'Lord Christ, that so to ransom me descendedst long ago
Out of thy Father's bosom, and in the Virgin's womb 2675
Didst put on flesh, oh, let my plaint out of this hollow tomb,
Pierce through the air, and grant my suit may favour find;
Take pity on my sinful and my poor afflicted mind!
For well enough I know, this body is but clay,
Nought but a mass of sin, too frail, and subject to decay.' 2680
Then pressed with extreme grief he threw with so great force
His overpresséd parts upon his lady's wailéd corse,
That now his weakened heart, weakened with torments past,
Unable to abide this pang, the sharpest and the last,
Remainéd quite deprived of sense and kindly strength, 2685
And so the long imprisoned soul hath freedom won at length.
Ah cruel death, too soon, too soon was this divorce, [corse!
'Twixt youthful Romeus' heavenly sprite, and his fair earthy
 The friar that knew what time the powder had been taken,
Knew eke the very instant when the sleeper should awaken;
But wondering that he could no kind of answer hear 2691
Of letters which to Romeus his fellow friar did bear,
Out of Saint Francis' church himself alone did fare,
And for the opening of the tomb meet instruments he bare.
Approaching nigh the place and seeing there the light, 2695
Great horror felt he in his heart, by strange and sudden sight;

Till Peter, Romeus' man, his coward heart made bold,
When of his master's being there the certain news he told :
  'There hath he been,' quoth he, 'this half hour at the
    least,
And in this time, I dare well say, his plaint hath still increast.'
Then both they entered in, where they, alas, did find 2701
The breathless corpse of Romeus, forsaken of the mind :
Where they have made such moan, as they may best conceive,
That have with perfect friendship loved, whose friend fierce
    death did reave.
  But whilst with piteous plaint they Romeus' fate beweep,
An hour too late fair Juliet awakéd out of sleep ;   2706
And much amazed to see in tomb so great a light,
She wist not if she saw a dream, or sprite that walked by night.
But coming to herself she knew them, and said thus :
  'What, friar Laurence, is it you ? Where is my Romeus ?'
And then the ancient friar, that greatly stood in fear, 2711
Lest, if they lingered over long they should be taken there,
In few plain words the whole that was betid, he told,
And with his finger showed his corpse out-stretchéd, stiff, and
    cold ;
And then persuaded her with patience to abide   2715
This sudden great mischance, and saith, that he will soon
In some religious house for her a quiet place,   [provide
Where she may spend the rest of life, and where in time, per-
    case,
She may with wisdom's mean measure her mourning breast,
And unto her tormented soul call back exiléd rest.   2720

But lo, as soon as she had cast her ruthful eye
On Romeus' face, that pale and wan fast by her side did lie,
Straightway she did unstop the conduits of her tears, [hairs.
And out they gush ;—with cruel hand she tare her golden
But when she neither could her swelling sorrow 'suage 2725
Ne yet her tender heart abide her sickness' furious rage,
Fall'n on his corpse she lay, long panting on his face,
And then with all her force and strength the dead corpse did
    embrace.
As though with sighs, with sobs, with force, and busy pain
She would him raise, and him restore from death to life again :
A thousand times she kissed his mouth, as cold as stone, 2731
And it unkissed again as oft ; then 'gan she thus to moan :
  ' Ah, pleasant prop of all my thoughts, ah, only ground
Of all the sweet delights that yet in all my life I found,
Did such assuréd trust within thy heart repose, 2735
That in this place and at this time, thy churchyard thou hast
Betwixt the arms of me, thy perfect-loving make ? [chose
And thus by means of me to end thy life, and for my sake ?
Even in the flow'ring of thy youth, when unto thee
Thy life most dear, as to the most, and pleasant ought to be,
How could this tender corpse withstand the cruel fight 2741
Of furious Death, that wonts to fray the stoutest with his
    sight ?
How could thy dainty youth agree with willing heart,
In this so foul-infected place to dwell, where now thou art ?
Where spiteful Fortune hath appointed thee to be 2745
The dainty food of greedy worms, unworthy, sure, of thee.

Alas, alas, alas, what needed now anew
My wonted sorrows, doubled twice, again thus to renew ?
Which both the time and eke my patient long abode
Should now at length have quenchéd quite, and under foot
　　　have trode ?　　　　　　　　　　　　　　　　2750
Ah, wretch and caitive that I am, even when I thought
To find my painful passion's salve, I missed the thing I sought ;
And to my mortal harm the fatal knife I ground,
That gave to me so deep, so wide, so cruel deadly wound !
Ah thou, most fortunate and most unhappy tomb !　　2755
For thou shalt bear, from age to age, witness in time to come
Of the most perfect league betwixt a pair of lovers,
That were the most unfortunate and fortunate of others,
Receive the latter sigh, receive the latter pang,
Of the most cruel of cruel slaves that wrath and death aye
　　　wrang.'　　　　　　　　　　　　　　　　　2760
　　And when our Juliet would continue still her moan,
The friar and the servant fled, and left her there alone ;
For they a sudden noise fast by the place did hear,
And lest they might be taken there, greatly they stood in fear.
When Juliet saw herself left in the vault alone,　　　2765
That freely she might work her will, for let or stay was none,
Then once for all she took the cause of all her harms,
The body dead of Romeus, and clasped it in her arms ;
Then she with earnest kiss sufficiently did prove,
That more than by the fear of death, she was attaint by love ;
And then past deadly fear, for life ne had she care,　2771
With hasty hand she did draw out the dagger that he ware.

'O welcome Death,' quoth she, 'end of unhappiness,
That also art beginning of assuréd happiness,
Fear not to dart me now, thy stripe no longer stay,   2775
Prolong no longer now my life, I hate this long delay ;
For straight my parting sprite, out of this carcase fled,
At ease shall find my Romeus' sprite among so many dead.
And thou my loving lord, Romeus, my trusty fere,
If knowledge yet do rest in thee, if thou these words dost hear,
Receive thou her, whom thou didst love so lawfully,   2781
That caused, alas, thy violent death, although unwillingly ;
And therefore willingly offers to thee her ghost,   [to boast
To th'end that no wight else but thou might have just cause
Th'enjoying of my love, which aye I have reserved   2785
Free from the rest, bound unto thee, that hast it well deserved ;
That so our parted sprites from light that we see here,
In place of endless light and bliss may ever live y-fere.'
    These said, her ruthless hand through-girt her valiant
        heart:
Ah, ladies, help with tears to wail the lady's deadly smart ! 2790
She groans, she stretcheth out her limbs, she shuts her eyes,
And from her corpse the sprite doth fly ;—what should I
        say ?—she dies.
The watchmen of the town the whilst are passéd by, [spy ;
And through the gates the candle-light within the tomb they
Whereby they did suppose enchanters to be come,   2795
That with preparéd instruments had opened wide the tomb,
In purpose to abuse the bodies of the dead,
Which by their science' aid abused, do stand them oft in stead.

Their curious hearts desire the truth hereof to know ;
Then they by certain steps descend, where they do find below,
In claspéd arms y-wrapt, the husband and the wife,   2801
In whom as yet they seemed to see some certain marks of life.
But when more curiously with leisure they did view,
The certainty of both their deaths assuredly they knew :
Then here and there so long with careful eye they sought, 2805
That at the length hidden they found the murth'rers ;—so
　　they thought.
In dungeon deep that night they lodged them underground ;
The next day do they tell the prince the mischief that they
　　found.
　　The news was by and by throughout the town dispread,
Both of the taking of the friar, and of the two found dead. 2810
Thither might you have seen whole households forth to run,
For to the tomb where they did hear this wonder strange was
　　done,
The great, the small, the rich, the poor, the young, the old,
With hasty pace do run to see, but rue when they behold.
And that the murtherers to all men might be known, 2815
Like as the murder's bruit abroad through all the town was
　　blown,
The prince did straight ordain, the corses that were found
Should be set forth upon a stage high raiséd from the ground,
Right in the selfsame form, showed forth to all men's sight,
That in the hollow vault they had been found that other night ;
And eke that Romeus' man and Friar Laurence should 2821
Be openly examinéd ; for else the people would

Have murmuréd, or feigned there were some weighty cause
Why openly they were not called, and so convict by laws.
　　The holy friar now, and reverent by his age,　　2825
In great reproach set to the show upon the open stage,—
A thing that ill beseemed a man of silver hairs,—
His beard as white as milk he bathes with great fast-falling
　　　　tears :
Whom straight the dreadful judge commandeth to declare
Both, how this murther had been done, and who the
　　　　murth'rers are ;　　　　　　　　2830
For that he near the tomb was found at hours unfit,
And had with him those iron tools for such a purpose fit.
The friar was of lively sprite and free of speech,
The judge's words appalled him not, ne were his wits to seech,
But with adviséd heed a while first did he stay,　　2835
And then with bold assuréd voice aloud thus 'gan he say :
　　My lords, there is not one among you, set together,
So that, affection set aside, by wisdom he consider
My former passéd life, and this my extreme age,
And eke this heavy sight, the wreak of frantic Fortune's rage,
But that, amazéd much, doth wonder at this change,　2841
So great, so suddenly befall'n, unlookéd for, and strange.
For I, that in the space of sixty years and ten,
Since first I did begin, too soon, to lead my life with men,
And with the world's vain things, myself I did acquaint, 2845
Was never yet, in open place, at any time attaint
With any crime, in weight as heavy as a rush,
Ne is there any stander-by can make me guilty blush,

Although before the face of God, I do confess
Myself to be the sinfull'st wretch of all this mighty press. 2850
When readiest I am and likeliest to make
My great accompt, which no man else for me shall undertake;
When worms, the earth, and death, do cite me every hour,
T'appear before the judgment seat of everlasting power,
And falling ripe, I step upon my gravë's brink,   [think,
Even then, am I, most wretched wight, as each of you doth
Through my most heinous deed, with headlong sway thrown
In greatest danger of my life, and domage of renown. [down,
The spring, whence in your head this new conceit doth rise,
And in your heart increaseth still your vain and wrong surmise,
May be the hugeness of these tears of mine, percase,   2861
That so abundantly down fall by either side my face;
As though the memory in Scriptures were not kept
That Christ our Saviour himself for ruth and pity wept;
And more, whoso will read, y-written shall he find,   2865
That tears are as true messengers of man's unguilty mind.
Or else, a liker proof, that I am in the crime,
You say these present irons are, and the suspected time;
As though all hours alike had not been made above!
Did Christ not say, the day had twelve?—whereby he sought
That no respect of hours ought justly to be had, [to prove,
But at all times men have the choice of doing good or bad;
Even as the sprite of God the hearts of men doth guide,
Or as it leaveth them to stray from virtue's path aside.
As for the irons that were taken in my hand,   2875
As now I deem, I need not seek to make ye understand

To what use iron first was made, when it began ;
How of itself it helpeth not, ne yet can help a man.
The thing that hurteth is the malice of his will,
That such indifferent things is wont to use and order ill. 2880
Thus much I thought to say, to cause you so to know
That neither these my piteous tears, though ne'er so fast they
Ne yet these iron tools, nor the suspected time,   [flow,
Can justly prove the murther done, or damn me of the crime :
No one of these hath power, ne power have all the three, 2885
To make me other than I am, how so I seem to be.
But sure my conscience, if so my guilt deserve,
For an appeacher, witness, and a hangman, eke should serve ;
For through mine age, whose hairs of long time since were hoar,
And credit great that I was in, with you, in time tofore, 2890
And eke the sojourn short that I on earth must make,
That every day and hour do look my journey hence to take,
My conscience inwardly should more torment me thrice,
Than all the outward deadly pain that all you could devise.
But, God I praise, I feel no worm that gnaweth me,   2895
And from remorse's pricking sting I joy that I am free :
I mean, as touching this, wherewith you troubled are,
Wherewith you should be troubled still, if I my speech should
But to the end I may set all your hearts at rest,   [spare.
And pluck out all the scruples that are rooted in your breast,
Which might perhaps henceforth, increasing more and more,
Within your conscience also increase your cureless sore,
I swear by yonder heavens, whither I hope to climb,   2903
And for a witness of my words my heart attesteth Him,

Whose mighty hand doth wield them in their violent sway,
And on the rolling stormy seas the heavy earth doth stay,
That I will make a short and eke a true discourse
Of this most woeful tragedy, and show both th'end and source
Of their unhappy death, which you perchance no less
Will wonder at than they, alas, poor lovers in distress, 2910
Tormented much in mind, not forcing lively breath,
With strong and patient heart did yield themself to cruel
Such was the mutual love wherein they burnéd both, [death:
And of their promised friendship's faith so steady was the troth.'
    And then the ancient friar began to make discourse, 2915
Even from the first, of Romeus' and Juliet's amours;
How first by sudden sight the one the other chose,
And 'twixt themself did knit the knot which only death might
And how, within a while, with hotter love oppressed, [loose;
Under confession's cloak, to him themself they have addressed,
And how with solemn oaths they have protested both, 2921
That they in heart are marriéd by promise and by oath;
And that except he grant the rites of church to give,
They shall be forced by earnest love in sinful state to live:
Which thing when he had weighed, and when he understood
That the agreement 'twixt them twain was lawful, honest,
And all things peiséd well, it seeméd meet to be,   [good,
For like they were of nobleness, age, riches, and degree:
Hoping that so, at length, ended might be the strife,
Of Montagues and Capulets, that led in hate their life, 2930
Thinking to work a work well pleasing in God's sight,
In secret shrift he wedded them; and they the self-same night

Made up the marriage in house of Capulet,
As well doth know, if she be asked, the nurse of Juliet.
He told how Romeus fled for reaving Tybalt's life,   2935
And how, the whilst, Paris the earl was offered to his wife ;
And how the lady did so great a wrong disdain,
And how to shrift unto his church she came to him again ;
And how she fell flat down before his feet aground,
And how she sware, her hand and bloody knife should wound
Her harmless heart, except that he some mean did find 2941
To disappoint the earl's attempt ; and spotless save her mind.
Wherefore, he doth conclude, although that long before
By thought of death and age he had refused for evermore
The hidden arts which he delighted in, in youth,—   2945
Yet won by her importuneness, and by his inward ruth,
And fearing lest she would her cruel vow discharge
His closéd conscience he had opened and set at large ;
And rather did he choose to suffer for one time
His soul to be spotted somedeal with small and easy crime,
Than that the lady should, weary of living breath,   2951
Murther herself, and danger much her seely soul by death :
Wherefore his ancient arts again he puts in ure,
A certain powder gave he her, that made her sleep so sure,
That they her held for dead ; and how that Friar John 2955
With letters sent to Romeus to Mantua is gone ;
Of whom he knoweth not as yet, what is become ;   [tomb.
And how that dead he found his friend within her kindred's
He thinks with poison strong, for care the young man sterved,
Supposing Juliet dead ; and how that Juliet hath carved, 2960

With Romeus' dagger drawn, her heart, and yielded breath,
Desirous to accompany her lover after death;
And how they could not save her, so they were afeard,
And hid themself, dreading the noise of watchmen, that they
And for the proof of this his tale, he doth desire   [heard.
The judge to send forthwith to Mantua for the friar, 2966
To learn his cause of stay, and eke to read his letter;
And, more beside, to th'end that they might judge his cause
He prayeth them depose the nurse of Juliet,   [the better,
And Romeus' man whom at unwares beside the tomb he met.
   Then Peter, not so much erst as he was, dismayed; 2971
'My lords,' quoth he, 'too true is all that Friar Laurence said.
And when my master went into my mistress' grave,
This letter that I offer you, unto me then he gave,
Which he himself did write, as I do understand,   2975
And chargéd me to offer them unto his father's hand.'
   The opened packet doth contain in it the same
That erst the skilful friar said; and eke the wretch's name
That had at his request the deadly poison sold,
The price of it, and why he bought, his letters plain have told.
The case unfolded so and open now it lies,   2981
That they could wish no better proof, save seeing it with their
So orderly all things were told and triéd out,   [eyes;
That in the press there was not one that stood at all in doubt.
   The wiser sort, to council called by Escalus,   2985
Have given advice, and Escalus sagely decreeth thus:
The nurse of Juliet is banished in her age,
Because that from the parents she did hide the marriage,

Which might have wrought much good had it in time been
    known,
Where now by her concealing it a mischief great is grown ;
And Peter, for he did obey his master's hest,   2991
In wonted freedom had good leave to lead his life in rest ;
Th'apothecary high is hangéd by the throat,
And for the pains he took with him the hangman had his coat.
But now what shall betide of this grey-bearded sire ?   2995
Of Friar Laurence thus arraigned, that good barefooted friar ?
Because that many times he worthily did serve
The commonwealth, and in his life was never found to swerve,
He was dischargéd quite, and no mark of defame
Did seem to blot or touch at all the honour of his name. 3000
But of himself he went into an hermitage,   [his age ;
Two miles from Verone town, where he in prayers passed forth
Till that from earth to heaven his heavenly sprite did fly,
Five years he lived an hermit and an hermit did he die.

    The strangeness of the chance, when triéd was the truth,
The Montagues and Capulets hath movéd so to ruth, 3006
That with their emptied tears their choler and their rage
Was emptied quite ; and they, whose wrath no wisdom could
    assuage,
Nor threat'ning of the prince, ne mind of murthers done,
At length, so mighty Jove it would, by pity they are won. 3010
    And lest that length of time might from our minds remove
The memory of so perfect, sound, and so approvéd love,
The bodies dead, removed from vault where they did die,
In stately tomb, on pillars great of marble, raise they high.

On every side above were set, and eke beneath,   3015
Great store of cunning epitaphs, in honour of their death.
And even at this day the tomb is to be seen ;
So that among the monuments that in Verona been,
There is no monument more worthy of the sight,
Than is the tomb of Juliet and Romeus her knight.   3020

¶ Imprinted at London, in Fleet Street, within Temple
    Bar, at the Sign of the Hand and Star, by Richard
    Tottill the xix day of November, An. Do. 1562.

TEXTUAL NOTES

IN these Notes I record the readings of the various editions and of the original, and note words which have been modernised in this edition, but whose original form is worth notice. Spellings retained for purposes of rhyme are pointed out, too. The numbers refer to the lines.

The spelling of the original is fairly constant, but one or two words, like *subtle*, possess quite a variety of forms. In the original the past tense in final *ed*, in which the vowel *e* is not sounded, is usually spelt *de*, as *preferde* (11), sometimes only *d*, as *indewd* (26), but there are a few exceptions, as *sowede* (79) pronounced *sow'd*. Those words in which the ending is spelt *ed*, as *compared* (12), are to have this final syllable pronounced fully; in these cases the *e* is accented in our modernisation. When the final sound of the past tense is *t* the word is usually so spelt, as *prickt* (72), but there are numerous exceptions due to the conventional spelling, as *touchd* (233) and *forsd* (32). In some cases, too, the usual verb-ending in *est* of the 2nd person singular is printed in full, where the elision of the *e* would be phonetically more correct. *See* Notes to lines 1423, 1457.

Brooke retained a number of old forms for purposes of rhyme, as *geast* (162) for the sake of *feast* (161), although he elsewhere spells *gestes* (185). In some words the *r* has to be trilled for a syllable, as *forborne* (1022). These cases are also noticed.

As was often the case, the old editors copied one another. Collier followed Malone and Halliwell Collier, but Hazlitt collated his text with Huth's original and avoided most of the old errors.   Daniel went straight to the original in the Bodleian, and printed the most perfect text, and our text is in the main taken from him; but the original has been referred to in dubious cases.   In collating with Malone I used his small separate volume of *Romeus*, printed in 1780, of which only twelve copies were taken off.   This does not contain many of the inaccuracies noted in Daniel's collation. As Halliwell followed Collier, and apparently corrected his text nowhere except in l. 2926, where he reads the obvious *them* for *rhem*, I do not give the results of collation with him.

M. = Malone; C. = Collier; H. = Hazlitt; D. = Daniel;
O. = Original.

9. betid.   O. *betyde*.

18. hair.   O. *heare*.

38. blood.   O. *bloud*.

43. gentle.   O. *ientyl*.

50. burned.   O. *boornd*.

89. whilst.   O. *whilest*, but monosyllabic.

96. yield.   O. *yeld*.

97. he run.   O. *he ronne;* C. *be.*   The *h* in O. is a defective type, hence the misreading.

98. sun.   O. *sonne*.

101. among.   O. *emong*.

116. booteth.   C., H. *bootest*.

118. sweeter. O., C., H. *swetter.*

129. veil. O. *veale.*

135. barren. O. *barrayne.*

144. fret. O. *freate.*

162. geast, retained for rhyme with *feast.*

163. thither. O. *thether.*

168. press. O. *prease.*

173. than. O. *then.*

174. maugre. O., D. *mauger*; M., C., H. *maugre.*

192. beholding. O. *behelding.*

201. perfect. O. *perfit.*

213. scarcely. O. *skasely.*

220. wrapt. O. *wrapt.* In O. the words *rapt* and *wrapt* are confused. *Rapt* (283) is Middle English *rapen*, to carry away, transport, and so is *wrapped* (O. *wrapt*), 483. *Bewrapt* (382), and *wrapt* (388), are used correctly. *Wrapt* (220) is a further confusion, which was very common, with Latin *raptus*, from *rapere*, to seize. .

226. limb. O. *limme.*

267. tender. M., C., H. *slender.*

269. hath. C., H. *had.*

284. quoth he. O. (*q' he*).

305. so. C. *to.*

315. seld. O. *sild.*

316. the own. D. conjectures *their* or *his own*—unnecessarily, *the own* being a good expression.

352. yonder. O. *yender.*

374. th' attempted. O. *thattempted*; C., H. *that tempted.*

381. subtle.   O. *soottill*.

396. subtle.   O. *suttel*.

398. befiled.   O., C., H. *befylde*; M. *defylde*.

416. my thought.   M., C., H. *my thoughts*; D. conjectures *methought*.

419. talked.   D.'s emendation *talkt*; O., M., C., H. *talke*.

460. reaveth.   O. *reueth*; M. *driveth*.

    lover's.   O., C., H. *loues*.

463. doth.   O. *both*.

465. hour.   Bracket in O., C., H. and D. ends at *hour*; M. has no bracket; here at *bower* (466).   *See* next note.

466. bower.   M., C., H., D. *bowre*; O. *howre*.

476. Aye.   O. *Ay*; M. *In*.

484. sudden.   O. *sodain*.

557. betimes.   C., H. *bestimes*.

569. lurk.   O. *loorke*.

575. of.   D. *o* , a printing error.

599. redeth.   O. *readeth*.

663. tail.   O. tayle.   *See* Glossary.

666. chat.   O. *that*.

667. six.   O. *vi*.

733. quoth he.   O., C., H., D. (*q'he*); M. *quod he*.

740. friar.   O. *fryre*, here monosyllabic; usually dissyllabic, as 2045, and then spelt *fryer*.

746. hours.   O. *howers*, here dissyllabic.

777. will we.   C., H. *we will*.

783. y-beat.   O. *ybet*.

825. bound.   O. *bond*.

846. fets.   O. *fettes.*

856. all.   C., H. omitted.

870. feign.   O. *fayne*; in 844, O. *fayne* is *fain.*

871. sprung.   O. *sprong.*

872. wrung.   O. *wroong.*

899. easily.   O. *easely*; but in 1202 O. *easely* is only dis-
syllabic, and we print *easely.*

911. blindfold.   O. *blyndfyld.*

919. Thus.   O., C., H. *This.*

926. dis-eased.   O. *diseased.*

940. turn.   O. *toorne.*

957. raked.   O. *raakd.*

985. gasp.   O., M., H., D. *gaspe*; C. *graspe.*

988. whom.   O., D. *whō*; M., H. *whom*; C. *who.*

1003. and.   M. omitted.

   fiĕrce.   O., M., C., H. *feerce*; D. *fee   *, an
error in printing.

1010. sword.   O. *swerd.*

   hath.   M., C., H. *had.*

1022. forborne; the *r* is trilled, making the word tris-
syllabic.

1051. plague.   O. *plage.*

1060. luckless.   O. *lookeles.*

1062. native.   O. *natife*; so also 1439.

1070. seĕr's.   O. *seers.*

1099. accursed.   O. *a curst.*

1110. abode.   M., D. *abode*; O., C., H. *abrode.*   *Abode*
is apparently correct, for Boaistuau has here *repos,* p. 57, b.

1119. weened.   O. *wend.*

1188. begun.   O., C., H., D. *begoone*; M. *begonne.*

1192. me.   O. *my.*

1202. easely, here dissyllabic.   *See* note to 899.

1204. held.   O. *hyld.*

1205. sits.   C., H. *fits.*

1258. lover.   O. *louer, louer.*

1322. with.   O., D. *w^t*; C., H. *w' sobs.*

1331. wishéd that he had.   O., M., C., H. *wished that he had*; D. reads *he* [*ne*] *had,* unnecessarily, I think : the original spelling, *wished,* shows that the word is dissyllabic and the insertion of *ne* destroys the metre.   The poet simply means that he (Romeus) wished he had been born earlier, so as to have avoided the troubles consequent upon his actual life-time.

1339. lasten.   C., H. *hasten.*

1344. Unconstant.   O. *Vinconstant*; C., H. *Uinconstant.*

1357. hour.   O. *howre,* is dissyllabic.

1389. gaol.   O, *gayle.*

1396. after.   O., C., H. *afther.*

1401. med'cine.   O. *medson.*

1423. mad'st.   O., etc., *madest,* but monosyllabic.

1432. ought'st.   O., H. *oughtest,* but monosyllabic; C. *oughest*; M., D. *oughtst.*

1452. may'st.   O., C., H., D. *mast*; M. *mayst.*

1453. Thither.   O. *Thether.*

1457. leav'st.   O. *leauest,* but monosyllabic.

1487. veil.   O. *veale.*

1491. skill-less. O. *skil les.*

1535. muët. O. *muet.*

1554. geason. O. *geyson.*

1561. That. O., C., H. *Thol.*

1574. dooms. O., C., H., D. *doomes*; M. *doome.*

1592. tyrannous, properly, dissyllabic. O., M., H., D. *tyrans*; C. *tyrant.* *Tyrans* is the abbreviated adjectival form (*tyrannous*).

1645. will be. O. *wilbe.*

1646. so. O., etc., *no.*

1657. bent t'obey. O., C., H. *bend tobay*; M. *bent to obey.* Lore. M., C. *love.*

1680. foreign. O. *forein.*

1684. no. D. conjectures *now.*

1693. his. O. *hip.*

1769. hears. O. *beares*; M., C., H., D. *heares.*

1780. Romeus', possibly not the possessive case, but nominative.

1782. truce. O. *trewe*; M., D. *trewce*; C. *trewse*; H. *trews.*

1799. had. M., C., H. *hath.*

1840. amazed. O. *amasd.*

1850. frailless. *See* Glossary. O., C., H., D. *frayllesse*; M. *skillesse.*

1881. Among. O. *Emong.*

1893. features. O., C., H., D. *fewters*; M. *featers.*

1905. lavas, as in 491, where O., etc., have *lauas.* Here O., etc., have *lauasse.* *See* Glossary.

1910. yield.   O. *yelde.*

1945. wrath.   O. *worth* ; M., C., H., D. *wroth.*

1954. Whenso they.   O., M., H., D. *When so they* ;
C. *When they so.*

1957. thy.   C. *the* ; O., M., H., D. *thy.*

1973. Unless.   O. *On lesse.*

1986. unfalsed.   O. *vnfalst.*

2003. th'end.   O. *thend.*

2050. had.   M., C. *hath* ; H., D. *had.*

2059. she.   O. *the.*

2088. friendship's.   O., H., D. *frindships* ; M. *friendship* ;
C. *frindship.*

2097. travelléd.   O. *trauayled.*

2101. beasts.   O. *beaste* ; M., H., C., D. *beastes.*

2106. sprite.   O. *sprete.*

2157. dieth.   O. *dyeth* ; D. conjectures *lyeth.*

2159. Thy.   C., H. *The* : O., M., D. *thy.*

2161. themself.   M., D. *them selfe* ; O., C., H. *himselfe.*

2188. guie.   O. *gye.*

2239. into.   O., C., H., D. *in to* ; M. *into* ; D. conjec-
tures *in so.*

2248. precious.   O. *pretious.*

2259. earl, dissyllabic, the *r* trilled.

2269. show.   O. *shewe*, rhyming with *rew*, 2270.

2270. their.   O. *theie* ; C., H., D. *their* ; M. *theyr.*

2310. dis-ease.   O. *disease.*

2313. approachéd.   O. *opproched* ; M. *aproched* ; C., H.,
D. *approched.*

2314. tempered. O., C., H. *tempted*; M. *temper'd*; D. *temperd*.

2324. she. O., M. *the*; C., H., D. *she*.

2339. She. C. *So*; O., M., H., D. *She*.

2351. I not. O., H., D. *not I*; M., C. *I not*.

2383. weighed. O. *wayde*.

2390. tender. M., C., *slender*; O., H., D. *tender*.

2401. arms, dissyllabic, the *r* trilled.

2429. shrieked. O. *shriked*.

2450. to. O. omitted.

2570. shew. O. *shew*, to rhyme with *few*, 2569.

2616. tomb. O. *toomme*, rhyming with *comme*, 2615.

2629. upright. O., D. *vpright*; M., C., H. *up upright*.

2682. corse. O., M., H., D. *corps*; C. *corse*.

2736. thy churchyard. O., H. *this churchyarde*; M., C., D. *thy*.

2811. might you. M., C., H. *you might*.

2816. bruit. O. *brute*.

2837. together. O. *togyther*, rhyming with *consider*, 2838.

2843. sixty. O. *lx*.

2860. still. C. *till*.

2905. wield. O. *welde*.

2921. they. C. *thy*.

2926. them. C. *rhem*.

2959. for. D. conjectures *or*.

2971. much erst as he. O. *as erst as*; C., H. *erst as*; M., D. *much as erst he*.

2984. press. O. *prease*.

3008. Was.   M., C. *Has*; D. says: "[NOTE.—This correction obtained from Mr. H. Huth's copy of the ed. 1562. The copy in the Bodleian Library from which Malone (followed by Collier and Halliwell) printed his edition, is defaced in this place, the *s* only of the word remaining distinct.]"

GLOSSARY

Accompt, account, 2852

Accompted, accounted, 1625

Alcume. This can only be meant for Alcmene, mother of Hercules, for the sake of whose love, Jupiter extended the night. *Cf.* Chaucer, *Troil. III.*, 1427 :—

> O Night, allas! why niltow over us hove,
> As longe as whanne Almena lay by Jove?

824

Astonne, overpower, stun, 2131

Astound, astounded, 2033

Atropos, one of the three Fates. *See* Sisters Three

Attaint, convicted, 2846; infected, 2770

Aye, ever, 84

Bare, bore, 2630

Been, are, 3018

Befall, befallen, 1060

Befiled, defiled; a rather uncommon and archaic form, superseded by *befoul.* Collier's statement that our instance is merely a printer's error for *defiled* is not warranted. 398

Behest, promise, 1884

Beseeks, beseeches, 543

Beside, except, 2354

Besiegen, besiege, the old plural form, 2089

Besprent, sprinkled, 1576

Bet, better, 600

Betorn, torn, 2422

Bewray, disclose, betray, 455

Bin, are, 743; been, 1093

Blear, blur, dim, 2292

Blin, cease, 379

Blindfold Goddess, Fortune, 911

Bliss, bless, 285

Blissed, blessed, 2633

Boccace, Boccaccio, the Italian novelist, 16; 394

Boot, avail, 1833

Boot, remedy, 1922

Brackish, salt, 1576

Brake, broke, 1699

BRAST, burst, 2441
BRICKLE, brittle, 1850
BRUIT, noise, news, 2816
BUT, except, 1643

CAITIVE, distressed or afflicted person, 2751
CAPEL's, Capulet's, 157
CAREFUL, full of care, 1484
CHILLISH, chill, 2388
CHOLER, anger, rage, 1505
CLEPED, called, named, 30
CLOSE, secret, 2336
CONVICT, convicted, 2824
CORSE, corpse, 1040
COULD, was able to do, 1159
COVERT, secret, 630
COVETISE, covetousness, 2581
CUPID, 782, 915, etc.; his brand, 1442; his whip, 606
CURIOUS, careful, 1895
CURIOUSLY, carefully, 2803

DAW, arouse, 2417
DEBATE, strife, 166
DEFAME, blame, ill-repute, 2999
DEPART, separate, 1224
DEPOSE, call as witness, cause to depose, 2969
DESART, desert, 710

DIDO, Queen of Carthage, who loved Æneas, driven to her shores by a storm after the fall of Troy. Mercury compelled Æneas to depart, and Dido burnt herself on a funeral pile. 391
DIGHT, dressed, adorned, 897
DISDAINFUL, indignant, 1931
DIS-EASE, discomfort, set ill at ease; common in Chaucer, 2207, 2310
DOMAGE, damage, 2858
DRAVE, drove, 1184
DREMPT, dreamed, 646
DRENCHED, steeped, 2352

EASELY, easily, 1202
EFT, again, 1295
EFTSOONS, forthwith, 1235
EGALL, equal, 33
ERST, before, 586; first, 2017
ESTATE, state, condition, 51
EYNE, eyes, 87

FALSE, turn false, 594
FARE, go, 2234
FATES, HEAVENLY, another reference to the Three Fates. *See* SISTERS THREE. 4

FEARFUL, full of fear, 1944, 2637

FELL, cruel, perfidious, 78

FERES, companions, friends, 101

FET, fetch, 1076

FETS, fetches, 846

FIELD-BED, a portable bed, likened to a field of war. Boaistuau has here '*vn lict de camp*.' Shakspere has a play on the same word in *Romeo, II.*, i., 40. 897

FILED, "*tongue* so smoothly *filed*," a common expression, occurring in Skelton, Spenser, and Shakspere. *Cf.* "His discourse peremptory, his *tongue filed*, his eye ambitious," etc. (*Love's Labour's Lost*,V., i.) 1017

FLAWS, sudden gusts or bursts of wind, 1361

FOLDE, folded, 216

FONE, foes, 1288

FORCED NOT, cared not, 74

FORCE, "I force it not," I take no account of it, care not, 860

FORDONE, exhausted, 1468

FORLORN, lost, 1204

FORTUNE, 1343, etc.; wheel of, 935, etc.

FRAILLESS, in the original *frayllesse*. The line may signify, "glass (hard as it is) is brittle (and breaks), but youth, even less frail, is frail too." 1850. *See* note to this line, Textual Notes. Malone's emendation to *skillesse* does not commend itself. [? "and frail as frail is youth." I.G.]

FRAUGHTED, fraught, filled, 1116

FRAY, frighten, 911

FRO, from, 2618

'GAN, began, 48

GEAR, stuff, preparation, 2585

GEASON, scanty, 1554

GEAST, guest, 162

GHASTFULLY, dismally, 2033

GHOSTLY, spiritual, 595

'GIN, begin, 1235

'GINS, begins, 237

GLEAD, fire, flame, 303

GLIST'RING, flashing, sparkling, 2404

GRAFFED, planted, 268

GRECIAN RAPE, Helen carried off by Paris, 2237

GRIPE, grip, 259

GRISLY, horrible, dreadful, 40

GUERDON, reward, 1042

GUERDONLESS, without reward, 338

GUIE, guide, 2188

HALT, from the French *hault*, proud, high-minded, 966

HAP, chance, fortune, 15

HAPLY, by good chance, 1469

HASTE AWAY, hasten on, 1924

HATH WRONG, is wronged, 1048

HEIR, heiress, 1880

HENT, held, 1808

HEST, command, 19

HIED, went, 1090

HIETH, hies, travels, 2256

HIGHT, was named, 223

HOLP, helped, 580

HORSES, tearing asunder by, 1902

HUGY, huge, 2053

HYMENË, hymen, rites of marriage, 2510. French, *hymenée*

IMPORTUNE, importunate, 2275

IMPORTUNENESS, importunity *or* importuning, 2946

INGRAVED, buried, laid in grave, 2648

INTOMBED, entombed, 2373

IT, used in the genitive, as in the folio of Shakspere, till superseded by the modern *its*. The form is retained here as appropriate in the language of the foolish old Nurse. 654

JENNET, a small Spanish horse, 723

JOICELESS, juiceless, dry, withered, 1139. Boaistuau has here, p. 58: '*mon corps espuisé de toute humidité.*'

JOVE, 1305

KINDLY, natural, proper, 2154, 2662

LASTEN, last, 1339

LAVAS, lavish, 491

LEECHES, doctors, 2455

LEGEND, legendary, of the nature of legend, 39

LET, hindrance, 2766

LET, prevent, hinder, 2621

LETHE'S FLOOD, a river of Hades, a draught of whose waters brought oblivion, 214

LETTETH, prevents, hinders, 1620

LEWD, vicious, evil, 14

LEWDNESS, baseness, 1959

LIGHTED DOWN, alighted, 2613

LIST, chose, pleased, 28

LISTED, had pleased or chosen, 232

LIVELY THREAD, an allusion to the three Fates, 501. *See* SISTERS THREE.

'LONGED, belonged, 2287

LORE, learning, 66

LORE, lost, 1813

LORN, lost, 115

LUCIFER, the star, 1704

MAKE, companion, mate, 2021, 2737

MARS, 916

MAUGRE, in spite of, 174

MEAN, means, 1561

MO, more, 597

MOON, WASTED HORNS OF THE, 153

MOST, "the most," most men, 2740

MUET, mute (*dissyllabic*), 1535, 1944

MURTHERING, murdering, 1145

MURTHERERS, murderers, 2815

NE, nor, 190; not, 130

NILL, will not, 300

NOULD, would not, 1996

NOVEL, new, 208

OCEAN, "Ocean to the sea of Ind," a reference to Ocean as the great water which surrounded the world, 877

OTHER, others, other people, 822, 1381, 2473

OVID, 394

PEISED, poised, 524

PERCASE, perchance, 2201

PERCHER LIGHT, large wax candle, 2318. (The Cambridge University Library MS. of Chaucer's *Troil.* has *percher* in Book iv., l. 1245, instead of the usual *morter*. *See* Skeat's Note to his edition, p. 492.)

PHŒBUS, the Sun; a name for Apollo, 228

PHŒBUS, steeds of, 920, 1254

PLEASURE, Mount of, and the pit of pain, 1672

PLIGHT, folded, 2635

PLIGHT, plighted, gave, 145

POISONED HOOK, wrapped in the pleasant bait, 388

PORT, appearance, bearing, 138

POST, "in post," in haste, hastily, 2532

PREAST, pressed, 2445

PRESS, throng, crowd, 2984

PREST, ready. Copied from Boaistuau, p. 48 b.: '*preste & appareillée de vous suiure.*' 314

PROPER, own, 513, 2082

PROVERBS :—

'Unminded oft are they that are unseen,' 206

The poisoned hook is oft wrapped in the pleasant bait, 388

Falsehood hides in cloak of Truth, 389

'There is no better way to fish than with a golden hook,' 712

Lost opportunities never recur, 891-2

Love's troubles last long, 1339

'Pleasures grow of sight,' 1660

'The thing that hurteth is the malice of his [a man's] will,' 2879

QUARIERS, small candles consisting of a block of wax with a wick in the middle, 836

QUELL, kill, 1233

QUOD, quoth, said, 633

RACE, people, populace, 248

RAMPETH, reareth, rageth, 1027

RAMPIRE, rampart, 1154

RAPT, carried away, transported, 283, 1095, 2239

RAUGHT, reached, seized, 263

REAVED, tore, or snatched away, 38

RECOURSE, return; *perhaps* visiting place, 2419

RECURE, recovery, 73

REDETH, counsels, advises, 599

REFT, snatched away, 2667

REPORT; her trumpet, 398

RESTINESS, sluggishness, 1756

RIVE, rend, cleave, 1192
RIVE, tear away, banish, 208
ROUND, whisper, 344
ROUT, crowd, 163
RUE, sorrow, 2814

SCANT, scarcely, 16
'SCAPE, escape, 1250
SEECH, seek, 2834. "His wits to seech," his wits wanting.
SEEK, sicken, 413
SEELY, fond, foolish, 122, 640
SELD, seldom, 315
SHENT, chidden, blamed, 648
SHOPE, shaped, 1030
SHROUD, cover, conceal, 1290.
SISTERS THREE, the three Fates, Clotho, Lachesis, and Atropos, who presided over the destiny of men. The first was represented as holding the distaff and as spinning the thread, and Atropos as cutting it. Very frequently mentioned by Chaucer. 23
SITH, since, 19
SKIES, turning, the revolving heavens, 1747
SKILLESS, without skill, 23
SKILLS, knowledge, ability, 571

SOWND, swoon, 847
SPRITE, spirit, 1109
STALE, stole, 2272
STAY, prevention, 2766
STEDE, stead, 1416
STERVE, perish, 134
STERVED, dead, 2462
STRAITLY, closely, tightly, 2635
STRAKE, struck, 234
'SUAGE, assuage, 2725

TAIL, posterior, with an implied pun on *tale*, 663
TANTALUS, condemned to suffer intolerable thirst in Hades, steeped up to the chin in water which he could not drink, 339
TARE, tore, 1291
TESTY, petulant, 1931
THESEUS, governor of Athens; he married Hippolyta (*cf. Midsummer Night's Dream*) and was met by a number of female suppliants complaining of Creon, King of Thebes. Theseus took Thebes and slew Creon, capturing there Palamos, and Arcite (*cf.* Chaucer's *Knight's Tale*). 198, 392

THRALLED, subdued, 2415

THROUGH-GIRT, smitten through, pierced (*Troil.*, iv., 627), 2789

TICKEL, unstable, 1405

TIDE, time, 1253

TILT, tilth, tillage ground, 786

TOFORE, before, 1919

TOOTING HOLE, spyhole, 450

TRODE, trodden, 2750

UNGRATE, ingrate, ungrateful, 2212

UNSHUT, opened, 2405

UNTIL, unto, 1910

UPRIGHT BEAM, "with upright beam he weighed," etc.; he judged without bias, as though weighing with level balances, 195. (*See* also l. 524.)

URE, use, 2953

VENUS, 917

VENUS' CHILD, Cupid, 782

VIAL, phial, bottle, 2149

WALT'RING, wallowing, weltering, 1293

WAN, won, 1332

WARE, wore, 1292

WARELESS, unwary, 220

WARELY, warily, 249

WAXEN, grow, wax, 1039

WEED, robe, clothes, 1620

WEEN, think, consider, 332

WEEPEN, weep (*plural*), 2473.

WELL AWAY, alas! 2409

WIGHT, man, person, 338

WIST, knew, 265

WITHOUTEN, without, 1735

WONE, dwell, 2497

WONES, dwells, 1963

WORTH, worthy, 2649

WOX, waxed, 209

WRACK, wreck, 808

WRACKED, wrecked, 1368

WRACKFUL, dangerous, 802

WRAPPED, carried away, transported, 483

WRAPT, seized, 220

WREAKFUL, revengeful, 2116

Y-FERE, in companionship, 2788

Y-FOLD, folded, 1319

Y-THRALLED, subjected, 1873

Y-WIS, certainly, 701

APPENDIX I

TABLE OF CORRESPONDENCE

BETWEEN

BROOKE'S POEM AND SHAKSPERE'S PLAY

THE numbers on the left refer to Brooke's lines. The right-hand side of the column is reserved for the parallels or references in Shakspere's text. For the Italian novels I used Chiarini's reprint; for Boaistuau, the edition of 1559; for Shakspere, Professor Gollancz's Temple Edition; and for Chaucer, Professor Skeat's Clarendon Press Edition, 1900.

The following abbreviations are used in Appendices I. and II.:

Br. = Brooke	N. = Nurse
C. = Capulet	P. = Paris
Cris. = Criseyde	Pand. = Pandarus
J. = Juliet	R. = Romeo
L. = Laurence	Sh. = Shakspere
M. = Montague	*Troil.* = Chaucer's *Troilus and Criseyde*

Argument

Corresponds to 1st Prologue[1]

The Text

2	1st Prol. 2		116	I. i. 223-4
25, 32	1st Prol. 1		137	I. i. 234
	I. i. first part[2]			I. ii. 87
41	I. i. 88		140	I. ii. 99
53	I. v. 69		145	*Cf.* I. i. 243-4
57	I. i. 174 *seq.*		155	*See* note[3]
	I. ii. 46-51		157	I. ii. 20
75	Not in Sh.		162	I. ii. 34, 67
92	I. i. 125 *seq.*		165	I. ii. 67
101	I. i. 166 (Benvolio)			I. v. 67

[1] In Br. the story commences before Christmas, 155; a number of days pass after that in which R. passes J.'s window, 449, till the lovers speak in the moonlight, 467. The following Saturday J. goes to shrift, and is married, 716, 768. All this may take us to the end of January. Then their bliss lasts for "a month or twain," 949; the fray occurs the day after Easter, 960. This takes us to April. For some while afterwards, but we are not led to believe a great period, J. mourns. C. then forces her to promise to wed Paris on a following Wednesday, 1973, and this, she tells L., is the 10th of September. On this day J. is found in a trance, but meanwhile P. is said to have spent many days wooing her, 2277 (*see* also 2312). It is difficult to reconcile these statements and dates, but the significant point is that in Br. the action extends over nine months. In Sh. the lovers meet on Sunday; they wed on Monday, pass the night together, and part on Tuesday morning. C. desires his daughter to wed on Thursday, but alters the day to Wednesday. She is then found apparently dead, and is buried. On Thursday night Romeo returns to her and they die together. The time of action in Sh. is, therefore, only five days, but the play concludes on the morning of the sixth. *See* also 1997.

[2] Sh. mentions specifically *Three civil brawls*, I. i. 96; not in Br.

[3] *See* note to Argument.

167	I. iv.		344	I. v. 130
183	I. v. 67-94 [1]		353	I. v. 138
198	I. v. 43		357	I. v. 140
204	I. v. 54-5		365-428	Not in Sh.
	Cf. Prologue IL, 3		388	Cf. Prologue II. 8
208	I. ii. 46		439	II. i. 1
216	I. v. 43 [2]		448	II. ii. [6]
233	I. v. 99 [3]		456	Cf. II. i.
246	I. v. 20, 43		457	II. ii. 75
249	I. v. 52, 95			III. ii. 10-15
254	I. v. 95 [4]		467	II. ii. 23
	I. v. 53			II. ii. 52
255	I. iv. 27, etc.		493	II. ii. 64
267	I. v. 102		499	II. ii. 50 seq. [7]
279	I. v. 95-112		518	Cf. II. ii. 23
319	I. v. 113		531	II. ii. 94, 143
321	I. v. 114 [5]		536	II. ii. 144
324-5	I. v. 120			

1 In Sh. T. rises in anger against R. but is restrained by C. (*see* Introduction).

2 In Sh. R. asks a serving-man, but he is not able to inform him.   R. afterwards asks N., I. v. 114 ; in Br. the person he asks is not specified.

3 Sh. does not inform us of J.'s sudden passion, but her words, I. v. 99, would lead us to believe that she has already noted R.   In Sh. she is far more reticent and maidenly than in Br., where she opens the conversation.

4 In Sh. Mercutio does not sit by J. ; his presence would, of course, have spoilt the beautiful lyrical confession of R. and J.

5 *See* note to 216.

6 Sh.'s contraction of the time of the action and his conception of R.'s love would not permit of this dallying and frequent passing.   *See* note to Argument.

7 Sh. discards these windy rhetorical declarations, and gives us instead outbursts of lyrical splendour.

541	II. ii. 150-3	631	II. iv. 109[4]
554	II. ii. 127, 147[1]	633	II. iv. 192[5]
558-62	II. ii. 189[2]	634	II. iv. 198
563	II. ii. 125-7	652	I. iii. 16-62[6]
565	II. iii. 1-30		II. iv. 211
581	IV. ii. 31, etc.	667	II. iv. 194
587	II. iii. 31	673	II. v. 1
596	II. iii. 51, 60		II. v. 18[7]
597	II. iii. 65	679	II. v. 38
599	II. iii. 82	684	II. v. 48
601	II. iii. 85	685	II. v. 49[8]
607	II. iii. 90	688	II. v. 70
609	II. iii. 91	703	II. v. 38, 56
613	II. iii. 93	716[9]	
623[3]		721-2	Not in Sh.[10]

1 In Sh. it is J. who yields herself, firstly, when R. overhears her, II. ii. 49, and secondly, before N. calls her away, II. ii. 147.

2 He says this in Sh. in soliloquy, after J. has finally withdrawn, II. ii. 189.   In Sh., J. promises to send N. to R. on the morrow to get the news, II. ii. 145 and 169.   In both Sh. and Br., J. sends N.

3 In Sh. Juliet confides in the Nurse in the interim between Scenes ii. and iv., Act II., while R. is at L.'s cell.

4 In Sh. she brings her man Peter with her; Peter in Br. is R.'s servant; Balthasar is R.'s servant in Sh.

5 In Sh. the wedding is to take place that very afternoon, *i.e.*, on Monday.

6 In Sh. this is mingled with news about P., who has already been promised J.   In V. iii. 76, R. thinks it is his man who has told him this.

7 In Sh. N. is not speedy; she is over three hours gone : II. v. 1 and 10.

8 Elaborated in Sh.

9 In Sh. the permission to go to shrift is obtained in the interim between Scenes v. and vi. Act II.

10 In Sh. (II. vi. 16), J. appears unattended.

745	II. vi. 1	955	III. i. 3-4
753-66	Not in Sh.	960	III. i.[6]
767	II. vi. 35[1]		Cf. I. i.
774	II. iv. 221[2]	961	I. i. 39
779	Act II. vi.—Act III. v.		III. i. 38
809-13[3]		962[7]	
815-6	III. ii. 34[4]	963	II. iv. 19-27
827	III. v.[5]		III. i. 38
830	II. ii. 66	999, 1007	III. i. 59, 89,
841	III. v. 1		169[8]
920	Cf. III. ii. 1 ; III. v.	1011	III. i. 71

[1] In Sh. we do not see this marriage ceremony ; it takes place immediately after II. vi.

[2] In Sh. R. himself tells N. to come for the ladder, II. iv. 199, within an hour of that present time, and before the marriage.

[3] In Sh. the ladder is procured between II. iv. and III. ii.

[4] Here Sh. has introduced the fatal fray with Tybalt, cutting out this meeting of the lovers at night and many subsequent ones (see note to Argument), and concentrating all their passion on the one night of meeting and parting, III. v., for which, in Br., see 1529.

[5] See last note : this meeting is cut out in Sh.

[6] In Sh. the fight occurs on the wedding-day, soon after the wedding. There are two frays in Sh., the other being in I. i.

[7] Sh. does not mention the Purser's gate, the scene being merely *A Public Place*. In Boaistuau, p. 546 : *la porte de Boursari*. In Sh., Mercutio, rash and bold, provokes T., and is villainously slain by him under R.'s arm. Sh.'s R., just come from his marriage, is not capable of the burst of fury which Br.'s R. evinces, and is stirred to action only after the fall of Mercutio.

[8] In Sh. T. is watching for R., III. i. 59 ; he has already challenged him to fight, II. iv. 6, consequent upon his words of threat at the banquet, I. v. 94. None of this is in Br. Cf. R.'s interference with Benvolio's, I. i. 71.

1019	III. i. 136[1]	1145	III. ii. 98[5]
1031	III. i. 177		III. ii. 90
1034	III. i. 137[2]	1149	III. ii. 100[6]
1039	III. i. 146	1184	*Cf.* III. ii. 123, 135,
	Cf. I. i. 80		137
1040	III. i. 154, 186[3]	1209	*Cf. 2 Gent.* III. i.[7]
1075	III. ii. 69[4]	1211	*Cf.* III. v. 70[8]
1113-40	III. ii. 73-85	1218	III. ii. 138

[1] In Sh. R. refuses T.'s challenge, III. i. 65, in a gentle manner. This enrages Mercutio, who attacks T.

[2] *See* notes to 962, 999, 1007, and 1019, Appendix I.

[3] In Sh. it is Lady Capulet who demands that R. should die.

[4] In Sh. J. hears of R.'s banishment from N., who learns the news while gone for the rope ladder.

[5] "Ah, cruel murthering tongue, murth'rer of others' fame,
  How durst thou once attempt to touch the honour of his name?"
In Sh. her reproaches are amplified by N., on whom she turns :—
    "Blistered be thy tongue
    For such a wish ! he was not born to shame."—III. ii. 90.
Two Gentlemen, I. ii. :—
    "O hateful hands, to tear such loving words !
    Injurious wasps, to feed on such sweet honey."
and II. vi. :—
    "Fie, fie, unreverend tongue ! to call her bad
    Whose sovereignty so oft thou hast preferred."

[6] "Why blam'st thou Romeus for slaying of Tybalt?
  Since he is guiltless quite of all, and Tybalt bears the fault?"
Romeo and Juliet, III. ii. 100 :—
    "But wherefore, villain, didst thou kill my cousin?
    That villain cousin would have kill'd my husband."

[7] "You are accounted wise, a fool am I your nurse,
  But I see not how in like case I could behave me worse."
Two Gentlemen, III. i. :—
"*Launce :* I am but a fool, look you ; and yet I have the wit to think my master is a kind of a knave."

[8] *See* note to l. 1794, Appendix II.

1230	III. ii. 140[1]	1287	III. iii. 119
1234	III. ii. 141[2]	1292	III. iii. 12, etc.
1239[3]			III. iii. 68
1259-64	III. i. 141	1297	III. iii. 44, etc.
	III. ii. 141	1315	*Cf.* III. iii. 52-70
	III. iii. 1[4]	1318	Not in Sh.
1267	III. iii. 1	1325	*Cf.* III. iii. 119[10]
	III. iii. 76[5]	1352	III. iii. 165
1277	III. iii. 79[6]	1353	III. iii. 109-13
1280	III. iii. 146	1381	III. iii. 122-34
	III. iii, 161[7]	1383-1480	III. iii. 108-
1283[8]			158[11]

[1] In Sh. N. promises R. shall come that night; not in Br. *See* note to 1280, Appendix I.

[2] In Sh. N. goes to L. between Scenes ii. and iii., Act III.

[3] N. does not threaten suicide in Sh.; *see* note to 521, Appendix II. Not in Boaistuau.

[4] Br. omits all mention of R. after the fray until he has lengthily described the dolours of J.

[5] Br. says this secret place was where L. had secreted his "fair friends" in his youth, 1273; and yet we are informed that he had travelled abroad for twenty years, when young, 2099. Sh. suppresses this "secret place," and refers to L.'s *study*, III. iii. 76.

[6] In Sh. N. does not arrive until after L. has told R. his fate; in Br. she arrives before.

[7] N. has already promised this in Sh., III. ii. 140; and it is she and L. who actually arrange this at the cell, III. iii. 159-61.

[8] In Sh. N. tells J. in the interim between Scenes iii. and v., Act III.

[9] *See* note to 1277, Appendix I.

[10] In Sh. R. has not railed on his birth, etc., as L. says, and S. here has followed his original in one place, while forgetting that he had not followed it in the other. *See* Appendix II.

[11] In Br. L. lays down the law; in Sh. L. reasons. Br.'s L. has the same sort of wisdom as all the seers of euphuistic books; *cf.* the prolix,

1443	III. iii. 15[1]	1713	III. v. 35
1482	*Cf.* III. v. 130[2]		*Cf.* II. iii. 1-6
1490	III. iii. 165	1715	III. v. 1-58
1496	*Cf.* III. iii. 173	1725	III. v. 35-6
1499	III. iii. 149, 169	1732	Not in Sh.
1504	III. iii. 152	1733	Not in Sh.
1507	III. iii. 146[3]	1736	III. iii. 149-54[6]
1529	III. v.[4]	1744	*Cf.* I. i. 125-61[7]
1546	*Cf.* III. v. 60[5]	1794	III. v. 70
1605	Not in Sh.	1844	*Cf.* I. ii. 7[8]
1662	III. v. 52		I. iii. 63
1668	III. v. 60	1849	Not in Sh.[9]
1695	III. v. 44	1857	*Cf.* I. ii. 9
1703	III. v. 7		I. iii. 69

classical death-speech of Sir John of Bordeaux, in Lodge's *Rosalynde*, pp. 2-6, "Shakespeare Classics," 1.

1 "Unto a valiant heart there is no banishment,
  All countries are his native soil beneath the firmament."
Cf. Richard II., I. 3, on Bolingbroke's banishment :
    " All places that the eye of Heaven visits,
    Are to a wise man ports and happy havens."

2 ". . . the conduits of his tears." *See* also 1805.

3 After this in Sh. comes Scene iv., in which C. and P. arrange for the marriage of J. and P. on the following Thursday ; in Br. P. is not mentioned until after the banishment of R. (*see* Introduction).

4 Br. goes through the greater part of the night's story as Chaucer does in his *Troil.*, IV. ; Sh. shows us only their passionate parting, III. v.

5 Very little of this talk between R. and J. is in Sh.

6 R. goes to Mantua between III. v. and V. i.   Here in Sh. follow immediately the arrangements for the wedding of J. and P.

7 In Sh. this sorrow of R. is reported by M. earlier in the story. *See* note to 1758, Appendix II.

8 In Sh. P. has already been promised J., even before the lovers meet.

9 *Cf.* l. 1881-4. In Sh. P. is at the commencement a suitor, begging against C.'s inclination, I. ii. 6 ; there is, therefore, none of this in the play.

1860	I. ii. 9	1974	*See* Appendix II.
	I. iii. 12 [1]	1992	III. v. 197 [4]
1890	III. v. 68, 105	1997	Not in Sh. [5]
1893	III. v. 114	2005	III. v. 231
	I. iii. 74, 77, 80-94		IV. i. 18
1905	III. v. 117	2007	IV. i. 44 [6]
1915	*Cf.* IV. i. 77 [2]	2015	IV. i. 46 [7]
1929	*See* 1849	2019	IV. i. 55
1945	III. v. 142-97	2023	IV. i. 54, 62 [8]
1962	III. v. 179	2035	IV. i. 68
1973	III. iv. 20 [3]	2045	Not in Sh. [9]
	III. v. 162	2048	*Cf.* IV. i. 47
	IV. i. 1	2065	IV. i. 93
	IV. ii. 36-7	2066	Not in Sh. [9]

1 In Sh. J. is 14 years old. In Boaistuau she is 18 (p. 64.)

2 *See* note to 521, Appendix II.

3 Thursday in Sh. is the day first arranged, but C. afterwards decides on Wednesday. (IV. ii. 24 and 37. *See* Appendix II.)

4 In Sh. C. *exit* alone.

5 In Sh. the time-compression brings C.'s insistence to J. that she should wed P. immediately after the parting of R. The leave-taking of the lovers, Lady Capulet's talk to J. about P., C.'s storming at his daughter, and J.'s going to L., all take place in a short space of time, in one single morning. In Sh., therefore, there is no mention of J.'s retiring. The introduction of P. at this point serves to keep him in the action. *See* also 2015 and 2277.

6 There is no confession in Sh., although J. pretends to go for that purpose.

7 In Sh. L. already knows it, having been told by P. *See* 2045, Appendix I.

8 *See* 1915, etc. In Sh. J. threatens to kill herself only if there is no remedy for her predicament.

9 L. does not leave J. in Sh.; his disappearance at this point would be most inopportune, and for this additional reason, perhaps, P. is made to

2069	IV. i. 1 [1]		2163	IV. i. 113, 123
2070 [2]			2164	IV. i. 115
2072 [3]			2167	IV. i. 117
2074	IV. i. 68		2168	III. iii. 150 [7]
2091	IV. i. 92		2176	IV. i. 121
2109	II. iii. 15		2187	IV. i. 122
2129	IV. i. 93 [4]		2194	IV. ii. 15 [8]
2130	IV. i. 94		2200	IV. ii. 17-22
2132	IV. i. 96		2234	IV. ii. 33
2134	IV. i. 101			IV. iii. 1
2145	Cf. IV. i. 71-6		2239-42 [9]	
2150	IV. i. 91 [5]		2244	IV. ii. 31
2152	IV. i. 103		2255	IV. ii. 44
2159	IV. i. 109 [6]		2257	III. iv. 20 [10]

have already told him the news.   In Br. P. afterwards begs to see J., and does so.   See 2263 seq.

1 In Sh. L. has already asked P. this.   See 2015.

2 Thursday in Sh.   See notes to Arg., 1973 and 1997, Appendix I.

3 See note to Arg.

4 In Boaistuau L.'s youth is not mentioned, as in 2097 and 2122, but we are afterwards told, p. 83 b, that the friar gained his knowledge in his young years.

5 In Sh. this is "to-morrow night"; see note to 1997, Appendix I.

6 In Sh. L. says the trance shall last forty-two hours, IV. i. 105.   In Boaistuau, p. 69, and in Struijs he says at least forty hours.   Painter followed Boaistuau.   It may be that Sh. got his forty-two hours from the old play (?), or that he arrived at it by a certain time calculation. Thus, if J. drank the potion at 3 a.m. on Wednesday, she would be due to awake at 9 p.m. on Thursday, reckoning forty-two hours.

7 In Sh. L. says this to R. at the cell.

8 In Sh. J. meets her mother in the hall.

9 In Sh. C. is already there arranging for the feast.

10 See note to 1973, Appendix I.

2258 [1]		2291	Not in Sh.[7]
2259	*Cf.* III. iv. 23 [2]	2299	III. v. 220, 237 [8]
2263	*Cf.* IV. i. [3]	2301	III. v. 215
2271	*Cf.* IV. ii. 25 [4]	2304	*Cf.* III. v. 217
2274	*Cf.* IV. v. 41	2312	Not in Sh.[9]
2276	*Cf.* IV. ii. 24	2313	IV. iii. 2
2277	Not in Sh.[5]	2316	IV. iii.[10]
2281	IV. ii. 1 [6]	2326	IV. iii. 3 [11]
2288	III. v. 240	2341	*Cf.* IV. iii. 20 [12]

1 *See* note to 1974, Appendix II.

2 Sh. gives a far better reason for neglect of display. In the play it is C. who decides to have little celebration, and because of the death of T.

3 In Sh. P. sees J. at L.'s cell. *See* note to 2066, Appendix I.

4 In Sh., of course, she does not do this; it was quite inconsistent with her character. The corresponding passage in Sh. is IV. ii. 25, where J. says:

> "I met the youthful lord at Laurence' cell,
> And gave him what becoméd love I might,
> Not stepping o'er the bounds of modesty."

5 *See* note to Arg.

6 In Sh., III. iv. 27, C. says he will have "some half a dozen guests," and for these, IV. ii. 2, he wants "twenty cunning cooks." This is due to Sh. following Br. in one place (ll. 2281-7) and inventing in another.

7 In Sh., IV. ii., N. is present when J. tells her parents of her new decision.

8 Shifted in Sh. to III. v., before J. goes to L., and found only in Br. and Struijs besides Sh.

9 *See* note to Arg.

10 In Sh. J. and N. go to select the clothes before retiring; there is no intervening time as in Br.: another compression. *See* note to Arg.

11 In Sh. Lady Capulet enters at this point, and J. despatches N. to help her mother in the preparations.

12 In Sh. the mixture is already made by the friar, IV. i. 93, *seq.*, and *cf.* 2129, Appendix II.

2344	IV. iii. 24 *seq.*	2431	IV. v. 48
2361	IV. iii. 24, 30	2445	IV. iv. 25
2365	IV. iii. 38		IV. v. 33 [5]
2380	IV. iii. 42, 52, 55	2448	IV. v. 41 *seq.*
2393	Not in Sh.[1]	2454	IV. v. 31-2 [5]
2400	IV. iii. 58 [2]	2455	Not in Sh.[6]
2402	IV. iii. 58	2474-7	V. ii. 4
2403 [3]		2487 [7]	
2405	IV. iv. 24	2488	V. ii. 5-6
	IV. v. 1	2491	*Cf.* V. ii. 9-10 [8]
2407	IV. v. 1-11	2493	V. ii. 11
2418	IV. v. 14	2494	V. ii. 10
2421	Not in Sh.[4]	2502	V. ii. 14 [9]
2424	IV. v. 19	2505	*Cf.* IV. v. 91
2427 [4]		2508	IV. v. 84 [10]

1 *Cf.* IV. iii. 50.

2 In Sh. she drinks thinking of R.

3 The day must dawn, in Sh., in IV. iv. *Cf.* l. 4.

4 In Sh. Lady Capulet enters the chamber on hearing the cries of N.; C. follows.

5 Sh., following Br., makes C. proclaim that he is speechless, but allows him also to indulge in clamorous lamentation. (Malone.)

6 In Sh. L. is one of the guests, and there are no doctors sent for; their place is taken by the friar. L. is not present in the poem.

7 In Sh. we only see him on his return to L., V. ii.

8 In Sh. the friar goes to seek out a fellow friar visiting the sick in the city, and the town officials, suspecting they were in a house smitten with pestilence, kept them confined there. V. ii. 9-10.

9 *See* note to 2611, Appendix I.

10 "And now the wedding weeds for mourning weeds they change,
    And Hymenë into a dirge;—alas! it seemeth strange :
    Instead of marriage gloves, now funeral gloves they have,
    And whom they should see marriéd, they follow to the grave.

2515	IV. i. 111	2567	V. i. 57 [3]
2521	IV. i. 111	2577	V. i. 59 [4]
2523	IV. i. 109	2578	V. i. 60 [5]
	IV. v. 80	2581	V. i. 75
2526	V. i. 17	2587	V. i. 77
2533	V. i. 12	2588	Cf. V. i. 79
2547	V. i. 24 [1]	2593	Cf. V. iii. 22
2557	Cf. II. iii. 75	2597	Cf. V. i. 33, 36 [6]
2562 [2]		2604	V. i. 25 [7]

The feast that should have been of pleasure and of joy,
Hath every dish and cup filled full of sorrow and annoy."
R. & J., IV. v. 84:

    " All things that we ordainéd festival,
        Turn from their office to black funeral:
        Our instruments to melancholy bells;
        Our wedding cheer to a sad burial feast;
        Our solemn hymns to sullen dirges change;
        Our bridal flowers serve for a buried corse;
        And all things change them to the contrary.'

1 Notice R.'s swift decision as to his future actions in Sh., as compared with Br.'s idea on the subject. *See* also 2789, Appendix I.

2 In Sh. R. and his man Balthasar (*see* note to 631) meet in the street, and R. sends him off for post-horses. V. i. 26, 33.

3 In Sh. R. already knows the poor apothecary, V. i. 37, and the man's shop is adjacent. V. i. 55-57.

4 In Br. R. offers fifty crowns of gold, 2577; in Sh. forty ducats, V. i. 59; in Boaistuau fifty ducats, p. 76.

5 In Br. the apothecary says, 2585, "this is the *speeding gear*"; in Sh. R. says, V. i. 60 : "A dram of poison; such *soon-speeding gear*," etc.

6 In Sh. R. and Balthasar (*see* note to 631) apparently leave together.

7 He sends Balthasar for the ink and paper before he sees the apothecary in Sh.

2611	V. iii. 24 [1]	2694	V. iii. 120-1
2612	V. i. 26, 33 [2]	2695	V. iii. 125
2614	V. iii. 21	2697	V. iii. 122
2615	V. iii. 22 [3, 4]	2698	V. iii. 128 [8]
2619-20	V. iii. 25 [5]	2701	V. iii. 139, 144
2623	V. iii. 23	2702	V. iii. 144 [9]
2628	V. iii. 43	2706	V. iii. 147
2630	*Cf.* V. iii. 87-8 [6]	2710	V. iii. 148
2631	V. iii. 91	2713	V. iii. 155
2641	V. iii. 119	2717	V. iii. 157
2643	V. iii. 91-115 [7]	2721	V. iii. 161
2661	V. iii. 97-101	2733	V. iii. 163
2681	V. iii. 155	2762	V. iii. 158-61
	Cf. V. iii. 113	2772	V. iii. 164
2686	V. iii. 120		V. iii. 169

1 Here in Sh. follows V. ii., where Friar John returns to L. and announces the non-delivery of the letter to R. *See* ll. 2474-2502.

2 In Sh. R. sends Balthasar to do this.

3 In Sh. R. and Balthasar (*see* note 631) have apparently left together.

4 In Sh. alone, P. and his page are already there when R. and his man enter. V. iii. 1.

5 In Sh., he opens the tomb himself after Balthasar has retired, V. iii. 48-9. R. in Sh. professes to be opening the vault to take a precious ring from J.'s finger, V. iii. 30. Note that J. herself had sent R. a ring in III. iii. 143.

6 P. at this point comes forward and challenges R. in Sh., and R. does not descend until he has fought and slain P., and goes to lay him in the tomb.

7 In Sh. R. makes his long speech before he takes the poison, and dies immediately after.

8 This, in Sh., includes an account of the killing of P., which Balthasar imagines he has dreamt. V. iii. 139.

9 In Sh. the friar finds P. too.

2789	V. iii. 170 [1]		2829	V. iii. 228 [6]
2792	V. iii. 170		2837-970	V. iii. 229-69 [7]
2793	V. iii. 158		2955	V. ii. 1
2799	V. iii. 170-1 [2]		2971	V. iii. 271 [8]
2800	V. iii. 172 [3]		2974	V. iii. 275
2806	V. iii. 182, 184		2977	V. iii. 286
2807 [4]			2985	Cf. V. iii. 292-5 [9]
2809	V. iii. 191-3		3006	V. iii. 296
2821	V. iii. 216-22		3013	V. iii. 299-303
	Cf. V. iii. 198 [5]		3018 [10]	

1 Notice how swift J. is to act in Sh. on realising the situation. In Br. she first makes lengthy speeches. *See* also 2547, Appendix I.

2 In Sh. the watch are led in by P.'s page. *See* note to 2971, Appendix I.

3 And P., too, in Sh.

4 In Sh. they are not put in a dungeon; the Prince enters immediately after the watchmen find the bodies: it is then growing morning (V. iii. 189), and the trial proceeds after the entry of the Capulets and Montagues.

5 *See* note to 2807.

6 In Br., as in Sh., Escalus is evidently the judge. *See* 2985, Appendix I.

7 In Sh. says L. :
> " I will be brief, for my short date of breath
> Is not so long as is a tedious tale."

8 And also P.'s page in Sh., V. iii. 279, who raised the watch.

9 There is none of this judgment and punishment in Sh., nor are we told of L.'s subsequent fate. Br. here simply follows Boaistuau.

10 In Sh. Montague says of J. :
> " I will raise her statue in pure gold."—V. iii. 299.

APPENDIX II

COMMENTS ON THE TEXT
SHOWING BROOKE'S USE OF BOAISTUAU AND
CHAUCER

[For the cases in which there is no corresponding passage
in Boaistuau for Brooke's lines or phrases, and where Brooke
must have borrowed from Chaucer's *Troilus and Criseyde*, see
notes on ll. 332, 435, 613, 645, 824, 920 (chiding Titan),
1077, 1080, 1287, 1291-7, 1325-48, 1353, 1381, 1403-7,
1537, 1703, 1744, 1750, 1756, 1758, 1767-70, 1928 (?).
For cases in which Boaistuau's prose has been altered or
modified in translation, through Chaucer influence, see those
on ll. 271 (?), 314, 457, 500, 909, 924. Similarities in
phrase or incident which are not due to borrowing by
Brooke and which go back to the Italian sources will be
found in ll. 98, 119, 137, 211, 521, 841, 891-2, 929-32,
1046, 1091, 1161, 1173, 1283, 1532, 1546, 1616, 1673,
1715, 1802, 1844, 2271, 2281, 2301, 2393. The apparent
influence of the lost earlier English play (?) is shown in
ll. 1287, 2291. The similarity between Chaucer and
Shakspere, pointed out in l. 2547, is doubtless the result of
the independent employment of dramatic irony in the poem
and the play.]

ADDRESS TO THE READER.

    . '. . . the mountain bear,' etc. An example of that curious natural history which became one of the characteristics of Euphuism. Sh. may have had this in mind in writing 3 *Henry VI.*, III., ii.:

> "An unlick'd bear-whelp,
> That carries no impression like the dam,"—

but the idea was common, and occurs in Jonson, etc. Turbervile, however, certainly copied Brooke in his Epilogue to *Epigrams, Epitaphs, Songs,* etc., 1570, p. 145:

> "The worst [of his works] he [the author] made
>   in covert scroll to lurk
> Until the Bear were overlicked afresh,
> For why indeed this hasty hatchéd work,
> Resembleth much the shapeless lump of flesh
> That Bears bring forth," etc.

    . 'the eldest of them.' Not very old: *see* Introduction, *Date of the Poem.*

    . 'the rest . . . awhile shall lurk.' We know of only one more: *see* Introduction, *Author of the Poem.*

THE TEXT.

    98. So with Troil. in his love-sorrow over Cris.:

> "This woful wight, this Troilus, that felte
> His freend Pandare y-comen him to see,
> Gan as *the snow ayein the sonne melte,*" etc.
>
> Troil., IV., 365.

Cf. also *Troil.*, I., 524, when Cris. is cold towards Troil., and Pand. says:

> "Thy lady is, as frost in winter mone,
> And thou fordoon, *as snow in fyr is sone.*"

Boaistuau, following Bandello, has here, p. 41 : [R] *se fondoit peu à peu comme la neige au soleil.*

119. Troilus is learned, too; *see* Note to l. 1381, Appendix II. Boaistuau has, p. 41*b*: *tu es bien instruict aux lettres.*

137. Pand. gives Troil., bereaved of Cris., the same advice :

> " And over al this, as thou wel wost'thy-selve,
> This town is ful of ladies al aboute ;
> And to my doom, fairer than swiche twelve
> As ever she was," etc.—*Troil.,* IV., 400.

162. Brooke alone in the old versions has this written invitation.

207-9.

" And as out of a plank a nail a nail doth drive,
So novel love out of the mind the ancient love doth rive.
This sudden kindled fire in time is wox so great," etc.

From Cicero, *Tusc.,* iv., 35, 75 : "*Etiam novo quidam amore veterem amorem, tanquam clavo clavum, eiiciundum putant,*" *cf.* Ovid, *Remed. Amor.* 462, "*Successore novo vincitur omnis amor.*" *Troil.,* IV., 415 :

> " The newe love out chaceth ofte the olde ;"

and *cf.* 422 :

> " The newe love, labour or other wo,
> Or elles selde seinge of a wight,
> Don olde affecciouns alle over-go.

Two Gent. of Verona, I., iv. :

> " Even as one heat another heat expels,
> Or as one nail by strength drives out another."

Rom. & Jul., I., ii., 46 :

> " Tut, man, one fire burns out another's burning,
> One pain is lessen'd by another's anguish " etc.

King John, III., i., 270 :
> "And falsehood falsehood cures ; as fire cools fire
> Within the scorched veins of one new burn'd."

Jul. Cæsar, III., i. :
> "As fire drives out fire, so pity pity."

Coriolanus, IV., vii., 54 :
> "One fire drives out one fire ; one nail, one nail."

This is the nearest form to Brooke.

Boaistuau has here, p. 43 : *l'amour qu'il portoit à sa première damoiselle demoura vaincu par ce nouueau feu,* etc.

211. Very common in *Troil.* See I., 416; II., 1-7; V., 638 : but in this case from Boaistuau, p. 43, " *Le ieune Rhomeo doncques se sentant agité de ceste nouuelle tēpeste,*" etc.

253. The only instance of *Romeo* in this poem, used here for purposes of rhyme, the usual form being *Romeus.* Painter generally spells *Rhomeo,* after Boaistuau, but has *Romeo,* p. 103/10 (Daniel's edition).

254. Boaistuau says of Mercutio, p. 44 : *vn autre appelle Marcucio* [Marcuccio Guercio in Da Porto, and Marcuccio in Bandello] *courtisan fort aymé de tous, lequel à cause de ses facecies & gentillesses estoit bien recue en toutes compaignies,* and goes on as Br.   Here R. takes J.'s Hand seeing that Mercutio has the other.

271. So Diomed in *Troil.* changes when wooing Cris., *see* v., 925.   J. again refers to this "changing of his hue," l. 418, *see* Note to that line.   Boaistuau mentions only, *sa mutation de couleur,* p. 44*b*.

314. In *Troil.* Cris. will only consent to love Troil. if it be in keeping with her honour ; she says this many times : and J. insists on the same thing, *see* l. 532 and Notes, Appendix II.   J. uses the same words as Cris., copied by Br. —

Troil., II., 480:

> "but elles wol I fonde,
> *Myn honour sauf*, plese him from day to day";

and III., 159:

> "she   .   .   .
>   .   .   .   seyde him softely,
> '*Myn honour sauf*, I wol wel trewely,'" etc.

In Boaistuau at this point J. says, p. 45*b*: "*ie suis vostre, estāt preste & disposée de vous obeyr en tout ce que l'honneur pourra souffrir.*"

332.

"Of both the ills to choose the less, I ween the choice were hard."

From *Troil.*, IL, 470:

> "Of harmes two, the lesse is for to chese."

393. "A thousand stories more, to teach me to beware."

From *Troil.*, III., 297:

> "A thousand olde stories thee alegge
> Of wommen lost, thorugh fals and foles bost."

417. *See* Note to 271. These outward signs of love are frequent in Sh.'s works. *Cf.* Ophelia's description of Hamlet in what Polonius calls "the very ecstacy of love," *Hamlet* II., i.; Rosalind's description of a lover, *As You Like It*, III., ii., etc. Boaistuau says here, p. 47: *Car i ay experimēté tant de mutations de couleur en luy, lors qu'il parloit à moy, & l'ay veu tant transporté & hors de soy*, etc.

427. *See* ll. 608-9, 1559.

435. Br.'s sunrises apparently come from *Troil.*, where there are several descriptions which he might have borrowed: *Troil.*, II., 54:

> "Whan *Phebus doth his brighte bemes sprede*
> Right in the whyte Bole," etc.,

i.e., in the White Bull or Taurus.—Skeat, p. 467. *See* Note to 1703.

457.
"And when on earth the Night her mantle black hath spread."

Troil., III., 1429 ::

> "O *blake night*, as folk in bokes rede,
> That shapen art by God this world to hyde
> At certeyn tymes with thy *derke wede*."

Boaistuau says, p. 47 *b*: *mais si tost que la nuict auec son brun manteau auoit couuert la terre*, etc.

R. & J., II., ii., 75:

> "I have *night's cloak* to hide me from their eyes."

III., ii., 10-15:

> "Come, *civil night*,
> Thou sober-suited matron, *all in black*,
> · · · · · · · ·
> Hood my unmann'd blood bating in my cheeks
> With thy *black mantle*."

500. Frequently mentioned in *Troil.*; *cf.*, III., 733, etc. In Boaistuau he says simply, p. 48: "*Ma dame*, . . . *ma vie est en la main de Dieu, de laquelle luy seul peult disposer.*

521. *Troil.* contains frequent instances of characters threatening to commit suicide, and Br. has several after this.

532. This point is brought out often in *Troil.*, *cf.*, I., 1030-6; II., 351-57. *See* Note to 314, Appendix II. But Br. follows Boaistuau here, who says, p. 48 *b*: *si vous pretendez autre priuauté de moy que l'honneur ne le commande, vous viuez en tres grand erreur*," etc.

566. Boaistuau says, p. 49 *b*: "*Ce frere Laurens . . . estoit vn ancien Docteur en Theologie, de l'ordre des freres Mineurs*," etc.

609. *See* ll. 427, 1559.

611. The day's delay not in Sh., because of the time-compression.

613. From *Troil.*, I., 1086:

> " Now lat us stinte of Troilus a stounde,
> That fareth lyk a man that hurt is sore,
> And is somdel of akinge of his wounde
> Y-lissed well, but heled no del more :
> And, as an esy pacient, the lore
> Abit of him that gooth aboute his cure ;
> And thus he dryveth forth his aventure.

645. " golden locks." As Cris. in *Troil.* *See* Note to 1077, Appendix II.

746. *pres d'vne heure* in Boaistuau, p. 51.

774. Boaistuau describes the ladder, p. 52 : *Vne eschelle da* (sic) *cordes auec deux forts crochets de fer, attachez aux deux bouts,* and adds that such ladders were *fort frequentes en Italie.*

800. *See* Note to 211, Appendix II.

824. Br. says that the lovers would have brought night over the earth if they might have guided the heavens like Alcmene. Alcmene, of course, had no power over the heavens ; it was Jove who prolonged the night for her sake. Now, Boaistuau has here, pp. 52-3 : *de sorte que s'ils eussent peu commander au ciel comme Josué fist au soleil, la terre eust esté bien tost couuerte de tres obscures tenebres.* Br., therefore, took Chaucer's lines, III., 1427-8 :

> " O night, allas ! why niltow over us hove,
> As longe as whanne Almena lay by Jove ? "—

said, too, in connexion with the lovers' meeting at night— and substituted *Alcmene,* or, as he has it, *Alcume,* for *Josué,* keeping, however, the context. *See* Glossary, and Note to l. 1758, Appendix II.

841. *Cf.* the meeting and embraces of Troil. and Cris., *Troil.* IV., 1128, etc.

891-2.

' Who takes not time,' quoth she, ' when time well offered is,' Another time shall seek for time, and yet of time shall miss.'

So Cris., at her final meeting with Troil. at night, says, IV., 1611 :

> " And thenketh wel, that som tyme it is wit
> To spend a tyme, a tyme for to winne."

Cf. also IV., 1283. Boaistuau has here, p. 53*b* : *Qui a tēps à propos & le pert, trop tard le recouure.*

909, 924. Probably from *Troil.*, III., 1310 *seq.* :

> " Of hir delyt, or Ioyes oon the leste
> Were impossible to my wit to seye ;
> But iuggeth, ye that han ben at the feste,
> Of swich gladnesse, if that hem liste pleye !
> I can no more, but thus thise ilke tweye
> That night, be-twixen dreed and sikernesse,
> Felten in love the grete worthinesse."

and 1331 :

> " For myne wordes, here and every part,
> I speke hem alle under corecioun
> Of yow, that feling han in loves art," etc.

Cf. also, II., 19-21 ; III., 1693. Boaistuau has, p. 54 : *que peuuent iuger ceulx qui ont experimenté semblables [delices?].*

920. So Troil. and Cris. are parted by dawning, III., 1415, and Troil. chides day and Titan, III., 1450, 1464. *See* Notes to 1756, 1758, Appendix II.

929-32. *See* Notes to 815, and *Arg.*, Appendix I. So Troil. and Cris. arrange to meet every night. *Troil.*, III., 1710 :

> " And whanne hir speche doon was and hir chere,
> They twinne anoon as they were wont to done,
> And setten tyme of meting eft y-fere ;
> And many a night they wroughte in this manere."

949. *See* Notes to 815 and *Arg.*, Appendix I.

1046. In *Troil.* it is Cris. who is exiled from her lover ; in *Floris and Blanchefleur* it is Floris.

1077. *Cf.* the actions and lamentations of Cris., *Troil.,*
IV., 736 :

> " Hir ounded heer, that sonnish was of hewe,
> She rente, and eek hir fingres longe and smale,
> She wrong ful ofte, and bad god on hir rewe," etc.

See also l. 2723.

1080. So Chaucer cannot tell Cris.'s plaint, *Troil.,* IV.,
799 :

> " How mighte it ever y-red ben or y-songe,
> The pleynte that she made in hir distresse ?
> I noot ; but, as for me, my litel tongue,
> If I discreven wolde hir hevinesse,
> It sholde make hir sorwe seme lesse," etc.

1091. Cris., too, throws herself on her bed to make her
lamentations. IV., 733.

1099. Br. follows Boaistuau closely here.

1161. Cris. faints similarly on the prospect of separation
from Troil. ; *Troil.,* IV., 1156 :

> " This Troilus, that on hir gan biholde,
> Clepinge hir name, (and she lay as for deed,
> With-oute answere, and felte hir limes colde,
> Hir eyen throwen upward to hir heed)," etc.

and IV., 1168 :

> " With sorwful voys, and herte of blisse al bare,
> He seyde how she was fro this world y-fare !"

1173. Troil. also swoons in his love-troubles, III., 1092 ;
and he is revived as N. revives J., III., 1114.

1283. So Pandarus arranges the final night-meeting of
Troil. and Cris., IV., 887 :

> " And semeth me that he desyreth fawe
> With yow to been al night, for to devyse ;"

and he says to Troil., IV., 1114 :

> " For which my counseil is, whan it is night,
> Thou to hir go, and make of this an ende."

1287. All this scene between L. and R. (1287-1507) is not in Boaistuau, and was taken by Br. from the earlier play and amplified from Chaucer.

1291-7. This is Troil.'s condition when he hears of his separation from Cris., IV., 239:

> " Right as the wilde bole biginneth springe
> Now here, now there, y-darted to the herte,
> And of his deeth roreth in compleyninge,
> Right so gan he aboute the chaumbre sterte,
> Smyting his brest ay with his festes smerte :
> *His heed to the wal, his body to the grounde*
> *Ful ofte he swapte, him-selven to confounde.*"

IV., 250:

> " O deeth, allas ! why niltow do me deye ?"

1325-48. From *Troil.*, V., 204, when Troil. is bereft of Cris.:

> " And there his sorwes that he spared hadde
> He yaf an issue large, and ' Deeth !" he cryde ;
> And in his throwes frenetyk and madde
> He cursed Jove, Apollo, and eek Cupyde,
> He cursed Ceres, Bacus, and Cipryde,
> His burthe, him-self, his fate, and eek nature,
> And, save his lady, every creature."

Cf. also III., 1072-6.

1353.

> "' Art thou,' quoth he, ' a man ? Thy shape saith, so thou art;
> Thy crying, and thy weeping eyes denote a woman's heart.
> For manly reason is quite from off thy mind outchased,
> And in her stead affections lewd and fancies highly placed :
> So that I stood in doubt, this hour, at the least,
> If thou a man or woman wert, or else a brutish beast.
> A wise man in the midst of troubles and distress
> Still stands not wailing present harm, but seeks his harm's
>   redress."

Pandarus reproves Troil. : so, *Troil.*, III., 1098 :

> "O theef, is this a mannes herte?
> And of he rente al to his bare sherte."

and Cris. says, III., 1126:

> "is this a mannes game?
> What, Troilus! wol ye do thus, for shame?"

The last two lines are evidently copied in *Richard II.*, III., ii. :

> "My lord, wise men ne'er wail their present woes,
> But presently prevent the ways to wail."

1361. From Boaistuau, p. 59*b*. *Cf.* the similar storm in Greene's *Pandosto*, p. 69, "Shakespeare Classics," 2.

1381. *See* also l. 1413. When Pandarus reproves Troil. sorrowing over his loss of Cris., he says, *Troil.*, IV., 1086:

> "'O mighty God,' quod Pandarus, 'in trone,
> Ey! who seigh ever a wys man faren so?'"

Cf. also *Troil.*, I., 991.

1403-7. *See* ll. 1470, 1546, 1668, and *cf. Troil.*, I., 848:

> "For if hir wheel stinte any-thing to torne,
> Than cessed the Fortune anoon to be :
> Now, sith her wheel by no wey may soiorne,
> What wostow if hir mutabilitee
> Right as thy-selven list, wol doon by thee," etc.

1532. Br.'s R. and J. resemble in almost every way Chaucer's Troil. and Cris. in this, their final night together. As R. and J. embrace and are mute, so *Troil. and Cris.*, IV., 1130:

> "That neither of hem other mighte grete,
> But hem in armes toke and after kiste.
> The lasse wofulle of hem bothe niste
> Wher that he was, ne mighte o word out-bringe,
> As I seyde erst, for wo and for sobbinge," etc.

Br. says R. and J. stood mute the eighth part of an hour; Boaistuau says *vn gros quart d'heure*, p. 60.

1537. So Cris. leans her head on Troil.'s breast, IV., 1149:
"But on his breast her head doth joyless Juliet lay,
And on her slender neck his chin doth ruthful Romeus stay."

> "'O Jove, I deye, and mercy I beseche!
> Help, Troilus!' and ther-with-al hir face
> Upon his brest she leyde, and loste speche."

1546. Such laments over the action of Fortune are a constant feature of euphuistic books, and exceedingly common in *Troil.*, but taken here from Boaistuau, p. 60. *See* Note to 1403-7, Appendix II.

1559. *See* ll. 427, 609.

1603. *See* 521, Appendix II.

1616. So Troil. wishes to accompany Cris. when the time comes for parting, IV., 1506:

> "I mene this, that sin we mowe er day
> Wel stele away, and been to-gider so,
> What wit were it to putten in assay,
> In case ye sholden to your fader go
> If that ye mighte come ayein or no?"

1668. *Cf.* 1403-7, 1470, etc.

1673. *See* l. 1504. So Cris. promises to return to Troil. in ten days.

1703. These sunrises seem to come from *Troil.; cf.* III., 1415:

> "But when the cok, comune astrologer,
> Gan on his brest to bete, and after crowe,
> And Lucifer, the dayes messager,
> Gan for to ryse, and out hir bemes throwe," etc.

This is at a parting of Cris. and Troil. *See* Note to 435, Appendix II.

1715. *Cf.* the last parting of Troil. and Cris., IV., 1688:

> "And after that they longe y-pleyned hadde,
> And ofte y-kist and streite in armes folde,
> The day gan ryse," etc.

1733. In Boaistuau he parts *acoustré en marchant estranger,* p. 62 *b.*

1739. *See* ll. 1504, 1673.

1744. No mention of R.'s sorrow in Boaistuau, the whole of the passage (1744-72) being made up greatly from Chaucer.

1750. So with Troil.: III., 444, 1535.

1756. *Troil.,* III., 1702:

> " Quod Troilus, 'allas! now am I war
> That Pirous and tho swifte stedes three,
> Whiche that drawen forth the sonnes char,
> Han goon som by-path in despyt of me,"—

but here he blames the sun for rising too early. *See* also his remonstrance with Titan, III., 1464. *See* next Note.

1758. Troil.'s condition during his separation from Cris. is R.'s, V., 659:

> " The day is more, and lenger every night,
> Than they be wont to be, him thoughte tho;
> And that the sonne wente his course unright
> By lenger wey than it was wonte to go;
> And seyde, 'y-wis, me dredeth ever mo,
> The sonnes sone, Phaton, be on-lyve,
> And that his fadres cart amis he dryve.' "

Barnaby Riche in his *Farewell to the Military Profession* (1581) says in his tale of " Apolonius and Silla," translated from Belleforest and coming from Bandello: " Siluio thus departing to his lodging, passed the night with verie vnquiet sleapes, and the nexte Mornyng his mynde ran so much of his Supper, that he neuer cared, neither for his Breakfast, nor Dinner, and the daie to his seemyng passed away so slowelie that he had thought the statelie Steedes had been tired that drawe the Chariot of the Sunne, or els some other Iosua had commaunded them againe to stande, and wished that Phaeton had been there with a whippe."

1767-70. So *Troil.*, V., 456:

> " These ladies eke that at this feste been,
> Sin that he saw his lady was a-weye,
> It was his sorwe upon hem for to seen,
> Or for to here on instrumentz so pleye."

1794.

" For time it is that now you should our Tybalt's death forget.
Of whom since God hath claimed the life that was but lent,
He is in bliss, ne is there cause why you should thus lament.
You can not call him back with tears and shriekings shrill:
It is a fault thus still to grudge at God's appointed will."

R. and J., III., v., 70:

> " Evermore weeping for your cousin's death?
> What, wilt thou wash him from his grave with tears?
> An if thou couldst, thou couldst not make him live."

Hamlet, I., ii., 70:

> " Do not for ever with thy vailed lids
> Seek for thy noble father in the dust."

Hamlet, I., ii., 101 :

> " Fie ! 'tis a fault to heaven;
> A fault against the dead, a fault to nature."

In Boaistuau N. says to J. on her grief immediately after the fray, p. 59 : " *Et si le seigneur Thibault est mort, le pensez vous reuocquer par voz larmes ?* " The above-quoted passage from Brooke corresponds to Boaistuau, p. 63 : " *& mettez peine de vous resiouyr, sans plus penser à la mort de vostre cousin Thibault, lequel s'il a pleu à Dieu de l'appeller, le pēsez vous reuoquer par voz larmes & cōtreuenir à sa volonté ?* "

1802. Cris., on being wooed by Diomed, affects to be mourning for her dead husband, V., 973. In Sh., III., v., 75, etc., J. simulates that her grief really is for T.'s death, thus differing from her open confession in Br. *See* also IV., i., 6.

1844. *See* Note to 652, Appendix I. [Troil. is afraid that Calchas will want to wed Cris. when she goes to him, IV., 1471:

> " Ye shal eek seen, your fader shal you glose
> To been a wyf," etc.]

1849. *See* Note to 1844. In Boaistuau, p. 64*b*, as in Bandello, p. 76, P. is called Paris, Count of Lodrone.

1862. The common complaint of fathers with a single daughter. *See* Gower's *Confessio Amantis*, V., 6764; and *cf.* Brabantio's words, *Othello*, I., iii.; and Leonato's *Much Ado*, IV., i., "Grieved I, I had but one?" etc.

1867. Notice how reasonable C. is here and in Sh., I., ii., 7-34, and contrast this with his later furious outbursts in both poem and play. Lady C. does not apparently follow her husband's request. *See* ll. 1890 and 1908. The discrepancy occurs in Boaistuau.

1928.
" And up unto the heavens she throws her wond'ring head
    and hands."
Cf. Troil., III., 183:

> " Fil Pandarus on knees, and up his yĕn
> To hevene threw, and held his hondes hye."

1973. *See* Note to *Arg.* and 1997, Appendix I. In Boaistuau he gives her till *Mardy*, p. 66, to prepare and consent, but the marriage day is Wednesday, p. 67*b*.

1974. *Villafranca* in Bandello. *See* Chiarini's reprint, p. 95. In Sh. Free-town is the prince's judgment-place, I., i., 109. *See* Note to 2281, Appendix I.

2099. *See* Note to 1267, Appendix I.

2129. *See* Note on Sir B. W. Richardson's mandrake in *Introduction*, and 2341, Appendix I.

2194. Boaistuau says she returned *sur les vnze heures*, p. 70.

M

2271. In *Troil.* Diomed woos Cris., banished from Troil., as P. woos J. here with R. banished, V., 120 *seq.;* and Cris. was thought in this manner to have given her heart to Diomed, V., 1050:

> "Men seyn, I not, that she yaf him hir herte."

2277. In Boaistuau he spends *several* days so, p. 71 *b.*

2281. *Cf.* the feast of Sarpedon, *Troil.,* V., 435 *seq.* Boaistuau says at this point, p. 71 *b:* "*Villefranche duquel nous auons faict mention estoit vn lieu de plaisance ou le Seigneur Anthonio se souloit souuent recréer, qui estoit à vn mille ou deux de Veronne, ou le disner se deuoit preparer, combien que les solennitez requises deussent estre faictes à Veronne.*"

2291. In Boaistuau the whole of this passage, 2281-2312, is missing.

2301. So Diomed tells Cris. that if she loves anybody in Troy, it is not worth the while, for nobody there can get out to reach her. *Troil.,* V., 874-889.

2393. Troil., separated from Cris., is subject to similar night-fears and misery, V., 246-66.

2403. *Cf. Troil.,* V., 274. [The day must dawn in Sh. in IV., iv.; *cf.* l. 4.]

2474. *See* l. 2163.

2487. In Boaistuau he is called Friar Anselme, p. 74. In Br. and Sh. alone is he called John.

2508. *See* Note to 2508, Appendix I. C., ordering the feast, says, IV., iv., 5:

> "Look to the *baked meats,* good Angelica."

A reversal of this change from wedding to funeral occurs in *Hamlet,* where the late king's funeral swiftly changes into the queen's wedding, and Hamlet says, I., ii., 180:

> "Thrift, thrift, Horatio! the funeral *baked-meats*
> Did coldly furnish forth the marriage tables."

2526. In Boaistuau, R. had sent his man back on his arrival at Mantua, *au seruice de son pere*, pp. 62 *b*, 75.

2547. Before R.'s man arrives he speaks of his sense of joy in words full of dramatic irony, V., i., 1 :

> " If I may trust the flattering truth of sleep,
> My dreams presage some joyful news at hand :
> My bosom's lord sits lightly in his throne,
> And all this day an unaccustomed spirit
> Lifts me above the ground with cheerful thoughts.—
> I dreamt my lady came and found me dead," etc.

Cf. with *Troil.*, V., 1163 :

> " ' Alas, thou seist right sooth,' quod Troilus ;
> ' But hardely, it is not al for nought.
> That in myn herte I now reioyse thus.
> It is ayein som good I have a thought.
> Noot I not how, but sin that I was wrought
> Ne felte I swich a confort, dar I seye ;
> She comth to-night, my lyf, that dorste I leye ! ' "

This is, too, when Troil., like R., is separated from his love. I cannot explain these two passages as being properly connected, and consider their similarity only as a remarkable coincidence. To his Troil. passage Professor Skeat says (p. 500) : " *Cf.* Romeo's speech in *Romeo*, V., i., 1-11 " : he, too, noticed the likeness.

2723. *See* Note to 1077, Appendix II.

APPENDIX III

BROOKE'S DEATH

In a letter from Henry Cobham[1] to Challoner, dated May 14, 1563, the writer says: "Sir Thomas Finch was drowned going over to Newhaven [*i.e.*, Le Havre] as knight-marshal in Sir Adrian Poinings' place, who is come over. James Wentworth and his brother John were cast away in the same vessel, on the sands near Rye, and little Brook and some other petty gentlemen." In view of the parallel circumstances and the dates, we are justified in believing that "little Brook" is our own Arthur Brooke, the poet. A fuller account of the shipwreck is given in Stow,[2] where we read: "For you must vnderstand that Sir Adrian Poinings being knight Marshall, vpon his return into England went not backe againe: and then was Sir Thomas Finch of Kent appointed to go ouer to supply the roomth of knight Marshall, who making his prouision readie, sent over his brother Erasmus Finch to haue charge of his band, and his kinesman

---

[1] *Calendar of State Papers, Foreign*, 1563, p. 338.

I am indebted to the kindness of Mr. R. B. McKerrow for this and the following reference.

[2] *The Annales or Generall Chronicle of England*, by John Stow, 1615, p. 654, col. i.

Thomas Finch to be prouost marshall, whilest he staying till he had every thing in a readinesse to passe over himselfe, at length embarqued in one of the Queens ships, called the Greyhound, hauing there aboorde with him besides three score and sixe of his own retinue, foure and fortie other Gentlemen . . . . and as they were on the further coast towards Newhauen [*i.e.*, Havre], they were by contrarie wind and foule weather driuen backe againe toward the coast of England, and plying towards Rie, they forced the captaine of the ship, a very good seaman,[1] named William Maline, and also the master and mariners, to thrust into the hauen before the tyde, and so they all perished, seuen of the meaner sort onely excepted, whereof three dyed shortly after they came on land. After this mischance, Edmond Randoll was appointed knight Marshall."

It would be possible with these and other particulars given by Stow to fix the date of the shipwreck with a fair amount of accuracy. From other records, however, it is possible to fix the date with absolute precision. Henry Machyn says in his diary:[2] "The xxj day of Marche tydynges cam to the cowrt that on off the quen's shypes callyd the Grahound was lost gohyng to Nuwhavyn; the captayn was Ser Thomas Fynche knyghtt of Kent, and ys brodur[3] and on of my lord Cobham['s] brodur," etc. And in a letter from Cecil to Sir Thomas Smith,[4] dated 21st of March, 1562[-3], we read: "Here hathe happened two dayes past a lamentable

---

[1] *Cf.* Turberville's lines quoted in the Introduction.

[2] *The Diary of Henry Machyn*, 1550-1563. Edited by J. G. Nichols, Camden Soc., 1848, p. 302.

[3] Brother.

[4] *Queen Elizabeth and Her Times, A Series of Original Letters.* Edited by T. Wright, 1838, Vol. I., p. 133.

chance. Sir Thomas Fynche being appointed to be Marshall at Newhaven in the place of Sir Adryan Poynings, taking shippe at Rye with thirty gentlemen . . . . were lost with the shippe besydes the Camber," etc.

We are then able to state definitely that Brooke was drowned with Sir Thomas Finch on March 19th, 1563, in the ship Greyhound near Rye.

ALEXANDER MORING LIMITED
THE DE LA MORE PRESS
32 GEORGE ST. HANOVER SQ.
LONDON ENGLAND

CPSIA information can be obtained
at www.ICGtesting.com
Printed in the USA
BVOW08s1434160717

489427BV00017B/353/P